REMEMBER TO DUCK

A TRIAL LAWYER'S MEMOIR

by

MIKE BOND

Printed in the United States of America

First Printing, 2014

ISBN-13: 978-0692274804
ISBN-10: 0692274804

About the author

Mike Bond is a trial lawyer and writer who lives in the Pacific Northwest. Mike completed a BA in Philosophy in 1975 at California State University Fullerton, a JD in 1978 at Gonzaga University Law School, and an LLM in the Law of Sustainable International Development in 2004 at the University of Washington School of Law. A frequent contributor to the Financial Times, Mike's other published work include:

Rebuilding the Citadel of Privity
Doing Business with the Tribes: An Indian Law Primer
    for the Design Professional
A Geography of International Arbitration
Case Study in the Use of Mediation to Settle
    Environmental Coverage
The Arbitration Clause in International Project Contracts
The Americanization of Carlos Calvo
The Standard of Proof in International Commercial
    Arbitration

For my father, Tom Bond.

I see my life go drifting like a river
From change to change; I have been many things—
W. B. Yeats

A university professor, writer, painter, speaker of four
languages, Scoutmaster, fan of Louis L'Amour westerns, and
the CEO of a Silicon Valley software company when he died,
he told me he always wanted to be
a trial lawyer.

Table of Contents

Prologue

Trial lawyers tell stories and this is a collection of stories about my life in court. *My Life In Court* (1961) is the title of a best-selling book written by Louis Nizer, a very successful trial lawyer in New York City. He died in 1994 when he was ninety-two years old. One of my first instructors in trial work told us in order to learn the trade we should either try twenty-five jury trials or read ten books by lawyers who tried cases. *My Life in Court* was one of the ten books on his list. Since then I've read those ten books and completed close to one hundred jury trials.

While the technology, trial consultants, and pretrial discovery that exist today were not available in Louis Nizer's day, the surprises he wrote about, the challenges and adventure of working with juries, judges, and witnesses, and the public interest in what happens in court cases remain as true today as they were in his day. Each of the stories that follow includes lessons, advice, and tips for the aspiring trial lawyer.

ᴧ ᴧ ᴧ

I visited a courtroom four times while I was growing up. The first visit was when I sat in on a traffic court for a Boy Scout merit badge. A Mexican fellow got up to plead his case, and he ended nearly every statement with "you know." Each time he said "you know" the judge would bark back at him, "No, I don't know." I remember thinking that judge was a real jerk. I've encountered jerk judges one or two other times but, by and large, our judges are good men and women and dedicated public servants.

For my second visit to a courtroom I was the defendant. One weekend while my parents were out of town, I took the family car and went surfing at Doheny Beach which was, as the Surfaris used to sing in *Surfer Joe*, "where the surfers all go". At fifteen I was unlicensed and had never driven before. I'd never surfed before either, and it seemed like a good time to try out these new activities. Everything was working perfectly until the drive home from what had been a great day of surfing.

A California Highway Patrol officer pulled me over, he said, for a tail light that wasn't working. I fibbed my way through the stop by telling him I had just received my license but forgot it at home. He bought that whopper and wrote me up for a bad tail light and driving without a license. The court appearance was thirty days later.

After a couple weeks of worrying about what to do, I told my parents, and we went to juvenile court together. It was next to the juvenile hall, which was surrounded by a very tall chain link fence topped with mean-looking barbed wire.

When it came time for my hearing, the clerk sent us into a judge's office. The judge, who sat behind a large and imposing desk, pulled a book off the shelf and opened it to a particular page. He handed it to me, commanding me to "read this." When I'd finished reading, I looked up and he asked, "Do you know what that says?"

I replied, "Yes, sir."

He asked, "What does it say?"

I said, "It says the punishment for auto theft is ten years in the state penitentiary."

"That's right," he said. "Are we going to do this again?"

"No, sir," I promptly replied.

"Good," he said. "The fine will be fifteen dollars." He told us we could pay out front.

My parents were not happy with me, but my dad did say he approved of the way I told the truth and took my licks like a man.

The third time I went to court was in Parowan, Utah. While I was in college my brother, Steve, and I were going to ski at Brian Head resort in southwest Utah. Steve owned a very hot two door red Oldsmobile Cutlass with a big motor and four barrel carburetor and I was driving. In those days the federal government reduced the speed limit on all freeways to 55 mph. We were doing about 65 mph when I noticed a State Trooper going in the other direction and he was looking at me. Sure enough, I watched him in my mirror slow down rapidly, complete a u-turn to cross over to my side, and come after us with the flashing lights on. I pulled over to the side and got out of the car.

My dad taught me early on that whenever you have an encounter with the police it will go much better if you pass what he called the attitude test. He advised me to answer the officer's questions, look him in the eye, speak respectfully, and sometimes he'll cut you some slack. Not this time. It was cold out that day and the trooper motioned me over to the passenger side and told me to get in. I opened the passenger door and got into his car, leaving the door open slightly, when I saw the radar screen on his dash said 64 mph. He asked me what we were doing and I said we were going skiing.

He said, "Follow me in to town." Parowan was at the next exit.

We pulled up in front of a residential house and all three of us went inside. It was the home of the local judge who convened court in his living room. Steve and I remained standing while the trooper stood at the doorway.

He said, "Judge, I got them on radar at 64 miles per hour. The car has California plates and nothing came back on them." I took that to mean he learned that our car was not stolen.

The Judge asked, "What are you California boys doing out here?"

I said, "Your honor, we heard there was some great skiing at Brian Head and we thought we'd check it out." Parowan was not far from where the Brian Head resort was located.

He said, "Is that right, the snow's pretty good this week I hear."

I said, "That's what we heard, too. I am sorry we were in a bit of a hurry to get there."

The judge said, "The fine is going to be $25."

I said, "That's not going to leave us much to ski, and we were planning on getting a hotel room on the hill tonight." This was a true statement as Steve and I were short on funds.

He asked, "How good is your word?" In the Boy Scouts we promised to be trustworthy, but nobody had ever asked me that question before, and I didn't recall ever being asked to give my word on anything.

I quickly replied, "Well, it's never been broken." The trooper snorted and left the room.

The judge said, "You pay me $10 right now and mail me the $15 when you get home."

I did as he asked. And going home we didn't put the gas pedal down hard again until we left Utah.

The fourth time I went to court was to obtain an order releasing a small blocked bank account. The account had been established for a settlement of a car crash during my first year of college after a driver crossed the center line on Pacific Coast

Highway on a rainy night in Huntington Beach and hit my car head on. My dad negotiated a settlement with the other driver's insurance company, and the insurance company put the settlement funds in a blocked account. I needed the money to buy a janitorial business I had my eye on and I went to court, filled out some paperwork, and gave it to the clerk. She took it in to a judge, who issued an order releasing the account to me.

⋏ ⋏ ⋏

Over the years I've come to believe there are only three requirements to be a good judge:

1. read what I have written,
2. listen to what I say, and
3. treat me and the others in the courtroom with respect.

I've been in many courts where the judge more than fulfilled these basic requirements and plainly showed he or she cared about the lawyers who appeared before them. Judge Tom Swayze in Tacoma used to invite us into his chambers on our morning breaks to have a Danish and coffee. Judge Sharon Armstrong would always greet us by name with a warm smile. But I've seen some doozies, too, like that guy who apparently didn't care for Mexicans in his court.

Once a judge stormed off the bench after telling me he didn't care what I had to say. We were about to argue the case to the jury, and I was in the process of entering my objections to the court's jury instructions, and he told me I had already said everything I needed to say in his chambers. As there was no reporter in chambers, I told him I needed to make a record for appeal. That angered him, and when he stormed off the bench I made eye contact with the court reporter and continued to speak. She helped me make the record we used on appeal.

The court reporter is often the trial lawyer's best friend and you should always take care of your reporter. Like lawyers, they're officers of the court. They make the record of proceedings that will be used in the event of an appeal or if there is a need to have an accurate record of what somebody said. The best reporters will clean up the transcript and eliminate the "uhs" and other grunts and groans that sometimes pass for ordinary conversation.

Plus, you can use a court reporter for other purposes. I sometimes use a reporter to take down the discussion with counsel during a discovery conference when I have a complaint about the other side's responses to interrogatories or requests for production of documents. Having a transcript prevents an argument later about who said what. Another time, in a medical malpractice case my psychiatrist client had pages and pages of notes that he took when he was treating the plaintiff. His handwriting was excellent, but he wrote in very small cursive and it was hard to read. I had him read the notes verbatim to a court reporter and during trial the judge allowed us to enter the transcript with his notes into evidence.

人 人 人

About halfway through my fifth year of college, I decided to set a future for myself. I joined the U.S. Marine Corps and applied to go to law school. Joining the Marines seemed like a good idea because I didn't have the grades to get into one of the first tier law schools. In 1975, when these notions came to me, it seemed there were already too many unemployed lawyers. Having a job waiting for me when I finished law school was one of the smartest ideas I've had.

I bought a copy of the *Prelaw Handbook*, which contained information about every law school in the country. For each school, the handbook included a table with LSAT scores on one side, grade point averages (GPA) across the top, and the number of applicants and acceptances for each combination of scores. Playing it safe, I found four schools where 100 percent of the applicants with my scores were accepted, and one of those was Gonzaga University Law School in Spokane, Washington. I had never visited Spokane, but my dad lived there once. I knew its location would be great for skiing, hiking and fishing. Besides, Southern California was losing its attraction and, as my mother used to say, I might have been wearing out my welcome at my usual haunts. I sent my application to Gonzaga in March and my acceptance arrived in April.

λ λ λ

I graduated from California State University at Fullerton two months later in 1975 with a major in Philosophy and I spent that summer at Officer's Candidate School in Quantico, Virginia. I had another connection to the Marines. My father was a Marine Corps officer in the 1950's and my younger brother, Steve, was born in Quantico in 1954. It was a homecoming of sorts. I was commissioned as a Second Lieutenant at the end of the summer. My plan was falling into place.

Marianne, the girl I'd been courting for four years, and I drove my VW Westphalia camper with hippie curtains and an eight-track stereo to Spokane late that summer. I don't know exactly what I was thinking because we weren't married, and I had planned to check into Desmet Hall, the campus dormitory where Bing Crosby stayed while he attended Gonzaga. For a few weeks Marianne slept in the VW Camper when she wasn't warming up my dorm room bed. A couple weeks after I started classes at Gonzaga, Marianne's father came to Spokane to take her home.

It was a lonely cloistered life at Gonzaga, founded by Jesuits, and at the end of my first year, I asked Marianne if she would marry me. Luckily, she said yes.

⋏ ⋏ ⋏

Before we were married that summer of 1976, I went on active duty with the Marines at the El Toro Marine Corps airbase in Southern California and that is when I tried my first case. It was a non-jury Summary Court Martial, the details of which completely escape me now.

I was assigned to work with Captain Stephen Billie Ray, who had grown up in Nebraska and completed law school in Tulsa, Oklahoma. He was one of my best first instructors. Every Monday at 1:00 p.m., the Marines who were arrested over the weekend came before a magistrate for what would be called a bail hearing in civilian life to determine whether they should be held in the brig or released back to their units pending the trial for their offense. Typically, these guys were arrested for minor crimes of fighting, drinking, or smoking dope, and they had a right to counsel. Steve and I would go over to the brig every Monday afternoon after lunch to see if we could obtain their release.

The magistrate, who also was the Deputy Staff Judge Advocate, kept a bottle of Maalox® on his desk. You could tell he was having a bad day when he reached for the Maalox®.

We would meet with these new clients and in ten minutes of questioning, Steve would learn the guy's life story and then use some of it to craft a pitch to the magistrate in arguing for his release.

In one case that summer I second chaired an administrative discharge hearing with Steve. Our client was a gay Marine who wanted out of the Marines. This was long before "don't ask, don't tell" and gay men were not welcomed. He had been a good Marine with high marks and we called his father, a senior executive of a department store chain, who spoke about how proud he was of his son's accomplishments in life. Steve persuaded the board to recommend an Honorable Discharge for our client.

By the end of that summer I knew I wanted to be a trial lawyer. The need to size up the situation, discover the key facts, and create an argument on the spot was exhilarating. As a philosophy major in college I knew how to argue anything. Trial lawyering put that talent to use and it was in the service of somebody who needed help. Besides, at the end of the day most of the lawyers in that office would retire to the Officer's Club and drink and tell stories. I wanted to be one of those guys.

人 人 人

In many ways, I believe my career as a trial lawyer has been unique because I've been blessed with many very interesting cases and clients. When I'm defending, it takes a lot to convince me that I have a case of liability. If my client is the plaintiff, every case seems to me to be one of liability and big damages. As a result I tend to try a lot more cases than most lawyers. That means I've lost my fair share of trials and some of these stories are about my losses. Any lawyer who says they never lost a case either has a bad memory or he hasn't tried very many cases to verdict.

Many of my colleagues along the way came to loath their career choice and many of them express dissatisfaction with their decision to become a lawyer. Not me. We had a saying in the Marines that "every day is a holiday and every meal is a feast," and I've learned that if you go through life thinking this way, good things will come your way. The stories that follow are among the many good things that came my way.

For some of these stories, I used transcripts from a deposition or trial if I had one. In some cases I used my notes from my old trial notebooks, and for the rest I used my admittedly fallible memory. But every one of these is a true story of my life in court.

Chapter 1

You Are in the Marines Now

During the summer breaks at Gonzaga Law School, I went on active duty and worked in the legal office at the 3rd Marine Aircraft Wing air base at El Toro, California. Because I had not yet gone through The Basic School, I didn't have any uniforms and I wore a suit and tie when I reported for duty the first time at El Toro.

The orders to report for duty always say to "report to the Commanding General." Following my orders carefully, I drove to the gate at the base, asked for directions and I found my way to the building with a sign out front that said "Commanding General" and parked my car. I navigated the hallways with a certain determination until I found a door that said "Commanding General." Relieved to have found the right office, I opened the door and walked in to find a ramrod-straight man with a grey, flat-top crew cut and a bronzed and weathered face of chiseled features working at his desk. The general wore a stack of ribbons on his chest that went up to his shoulder and two gleaming stars on each shirt lapel. He looked up from his desk and peered at me with sparkling blue eyes.

Fearing nothing, I walked up to the front of his desk, snapped to erect attention, and in a bold voice said, "Lieutenant Bond, reporting for duty, sir!"

The General seemed a little startled and amused by this apparition in civilian clothes that had suddenly appeared in his office through a door that was never used. After inquiring into exactly who the hell I was and what the hell I was doing there, he hollered for the First Sergeant to come and take care of me.

Outside, the First Sergeant looked over my paperwork and took me aside. Speaking softly so as not to embarrass the young lieutenant in front of the other men, he told me that the next time it would be better if I would come through the front door to the front desk and check in with the Admin Clerk. He also suggested that I get over to the supply building and purchase some uniforms as soon as possible, Sir!

⅄ ⅄ ⅄

After graduating from law school and passing the bar exam, Marianne and I left Spokane and drove to the East Coast, where I completed eight months of training at The Basic School, at Quantico, Virginia, and the Naval Justice School at Newport, Rhode Island.

While at the Naval Justice School, in addition to learning about military law and procedure, we practiced examining witnesses and making opening statements and closing arguments. We recorded our arguments on video tape for a group critique afterward. The first time you see yourself on video is a sobering but helpful experience. During a trial, the jurors watch your every movement and it is good to know what they are seeing when they watch you. Only very few of us are as attractive or as cleaver or as smooth as we think. Seeing yourself on tape helps you become comfortable with how you look and act, and that is probably one of the most important tips to being a great trial lawyer. Be who and what you are, not somebody else. Although jurors come to court hoping they're going to see Perry Mason or Atticus Finch or one of the stars in *LA Law* or *Boston Legal* at work, they love authenticity, and if you're comfortable in your skin, they can tell.

One of the instructors at Naval Justice School told us about Louis Nizer's book, which is full of examples of things that happened in his trials, all of which seemed to be high profile, bet-the-company kinds of cases.

入 入 入

After completing training, we reported for duty at the Marine Corps Recruit Depot in San Diego, California. This is one of two Marine Corps boot camps where young men are trained to become enlisted Marines. The other boot camp is at Parris Island, South Carolina, where women are also trained to become Marines. At this point in my budding career as a Marine Corps lawyer I was – as we learned to say at Officer's Candidate School – a "highly motivated, high-stepping, highly educated, hard charging soldier of the sea," and I was now burdened with the added disability of being a full-fledged lawyer, eager to get my first client out of a jam.

I was armed with the Uniform Code of Military Justice (UCMJ) which is the substantive and procedural law that applies to all service members. The United States Supreme Court cited the UCMJ in the *Miranda* decision when the Court adopted the rights of those accused of crime to be informed about the Constitutional right to remain silent. Many argue today that the panoply of rights and procedures under the UCMJ would be more than adequate to address the handling of the detainees now held at Guantanamo, Cuba.

In those days, when a Marine was charged with a minor offense that his Company Commander would deal with, he had a right to consult counsel before the Commander could hold what was called a "non judicial punishment" hearing. With a few exceptions, the only Marines who ever exercised that right at boot camp were recruits. These were young men who decided – shortly after getting off the bus after flying all night from a small town, receiving a very short haircut and the first seriously loud yelling at – that they made a big mistake and would just as soon prefer to go back home. But because they had signed a contract and had already cost the government some money, it wasn't as easy as raising your hand and saying, "Excuse me, Sir, can I go home now?"

I was always intrigued by the difference in training philosophy between the officers and enlisted personnel. From the minute we got off the bus at Officer's Candidate School in Quantico, our drill instructors were up close in our faces, challenging us loudly and punctuated sometimes with sprays of spittle to go home just as soon as we asked. They called it "drop on request" or DOR. On the surface it seemed like an effective way to motivate a young man to reach a little higher in life and not take the easy way out. After all, who wants to be a quitter? But for well thought out reasons the enlisted recruits were never given an easy way out.

Those recruits at boot camp who had second thoughts about joining the Marines would create some disturbance or be disrespectful or try to get in trouble and they would deliberately get themselves charged with a minor crime under the UCMJ. My father, who was also a Marine Corps officer and once had been the Executive Officer of the Marine Barracks at the U.S. Naval Brig at Yokosuka, Japan, told me that in his day they referred to the "UCMJ" as the Uniform Coddling of Military Juveniles. As a result of some soft headed thinking, in my era they received free legal assistance before they were convicted and punished.

During the first few weeks of my first real job working as a lawyer at the Recruit Depot in San Diego, I would come to work in the morning and find six to ten freshly shorn young men lined up outside the door to my office, called a "hatch", waiting to see their lawyer. They had been charged with a crime and wanted to consult with counsel about their legal rights before submitting to non-judicial punishment. And I would bring them in one at time, sit them down, and try to listen – often through torrents of tears – to their tales of woe. Every one of these once tough Marine recruits, many of them big, strong fellows, would just cry their eyes out, begging me to do something to help them get home.

Instead of doing any real legal work, I was a camp counselor and psychologist who had no training whatsoever in those arts. My job I learned quickly was to provide a safe place of refuge, where, in as calm and unthreatening a voice as I could muster, I would try to reassure them that it wasn't so bad, there was a reason why they wanted to join, and that in a few months they would be glad they had stuck it out. All the legal rights in the world were of no use in this situation. The rules of evidence and procedure were not in play. When they appeared for Non Judicial Punishment, they could exercise their right to remain silent and catch hell, or they could try to defend their conduct and catch hell, or they could suck it up and get with the program. I knew more yelling by me wasn't going to be productive. These guys didn't need an attorney; they needed a coach. They needed encouragement, not more criticism, and more often than not it worked.

I learned from this experience a lesson that served me well in the future: our clients often need counseling more than they need legal advice. By becoming lawyers, we're granted special respect, and with that respect come expectations that we are wise and in possession of worldly experience that we can bring to bear on our client's problems. Sometimes these assumptions are true, but more often, especially just starting out a lawyer has not had the opportunity to acquire worldly wisdom. From our clients we learn about personal disasters that could not have been dreamt up. Often they have gotten themselves so wrapped up around the axle with trouble that we have no idea what to say or do, though we quickly learn to find words that help. And you will be amazed at what you can get away with if you project the kind of bold confidence that Lieutenant Bond showed that first morning when he stood before that two-star general.

⋏ ⋏ ⋏

After breaking me in as a camp counselor, the boss began to give me some trial work, almost all of which involved allegations that a drill instructor had abused a recruit. For the defense attorney, a drill instructor is one of the best possible clients. He was carefully selected for the job and had a stellar career up to that point with commendations from high-ranking officers and meritorious promotions along the way. To a man these drill instructors have never been in trouble before. Often you could find a high-ranking officer who would come to testify as a character witness for the defendant. More than once I found a former superior officer with combat experience who would come testify as a character witness for my client and say something like, "I don't care what you do here but he is the one I want beside me in a fight. When you are through with the Defendant, please send him back to my unit."

The UCMJ provides for a right to a jury trial, and the prosecution and defense are each granted challenges for cause and one preemptory challenge, which can be used to shape the jury. A challenge for cause under the UCMJ exists where the juror was part of the investigation of the case, or will be a witness, or has formed a positive and definite opinion as to the guilt or innocence of the accused, or has such a strongly held belief about an issue that he or she cannot impartially consider the evidence. There is no limit on the number of challenges for cause. A peremptory challenge does not require any reason, and whatever reason the lawyer wants to use need not be stated. Under the UCMJ, each side gets one peremptory challenge.

While the process is commonly called picking a jury, the reality is you do not pick a jury, you *unpick* the jury from the pool or venire that is presented to you. As in civilian practice, the trial lawyer is presented with a venire of potential jurors. In the civilian world the venire usually comes from voter registration lists or driver license rolls, and usually a reasonably diverse selection of the community is called in for jury duty. The trial lawyer's job is to ask the questions that help you decide when to remove those who don't fit the way you are thinking about the case. Maybe the juror has fixed ideas in the wrong direction about an issue that is key to your case. The prosecution prefers hard asses while the defense prefers someone who might have more empathy where your client has a story to tell. You use your *challenges for cause* or *peremptory challenges* to excuse jurors from serving on the case.

入 入 入

When I left the Marine Corps, I went to work for an insurance defense law firm that needed lawyers with trial experience. I read up on every book on civilian trial practice in the law firm library. The practice guides said that jurors from certain ethnic groups, such as Scandinavians, were better suited than others because they would naturally be more skeptical of plaintiff claims. The treatises counseled to avoid jurors originating from the southern Mediterranean because they're too emotional. These theories apparently go back a couple of centuries to Montesquieu, a French philosopher who in 1748 argued that warmer climates made individuals more passionate, while cold weather made them less prone to emotions. I never saw any studies to support these engrained assumptions.

I don't recall reading that race or gender should be taken into account, but in the right case this was clearly one of the tools in the trial lawyer's tool kit. Today in all jurisdictions using a peremptory challenge to remove a potential juror on account of their race would be grounds for reversal if the lawyer doing it is caught and fails to state a race neutral basis for the challenge. That is clearly the law in criminal cases following the Supreme Court's decision in *Batson vs. Kentucky*, 476 U.S. 79 (1986). This prohibition was extended to gender-based challenges in *J.E.B. vs. Alabama*, 511 U.S. 127 (1994). The Ninth Circuit Court of Appeals recently adopted the rule to bar peremptory challenges based on sexual orientation. Before long these rules likely will be applied in all civil cases. The theory seems to be that the rights of the parties at trial are less important than the interests of society in general, or the justice system, or the rights of folks called for jury duty.

We can all agree, I believe, that someone whose life is interrupted by a summons for jury duty should not be subjected to prejudice or discrimination on account of their race or gender or national origin or sexual orientation. But as an advocate for one of the parties at a trial, I confess I am conflicted about the competing values in that equation.

I can imagine a scenario in which a potential juror says enough to overcome a challenge for cause. Many times, the trial judge will try to rehabilitate a problematic juror by asking him or her, "Yes, but will you be fair?" Sometimes I'll ask the juror, "does that mean you'll give my client a fair trial before you hang him?" That usually gets a laugh and it may cause some jurors to recognize the problem of bringing preconceived notions to the task of judging the merits of the case. We all do it. Even when they say "Yes, of course I can be fair," in view of my client's race, gender, or orientation, the juror who for one reason or another isn't going to be able to give the client the shake I want should be asked to sit on another jury. Then again, maybe I'll want a juror's bias or prejudice to work in my client's favor. Is that wrong?

⅄ ⅄ ⅄

In one wrongful death trial arising from a landslide, during pretrial rulings the judge had agreed to a jury view of the hillside where the slide occurred. The parties, lawyers, judge and jury were going to take a bus out to see what could be seen on the hillside. In the trial of the case, we were going to use literally hundreds of photographs, engineering drawings, and an expensive scale model of the hillside. During jury selection, a blind man was called into the box of potential jurors. All the other lawyers tiptoed around the issue, but when my turn came, I said to the prospective juror, "Sir, I noticed you used a red tipped cane when came into the courtroom. What is the condition of your vision?"

He said, "I am totally blind."

I said, "We are going to have in evidence hundreds of photographs, engineering drawings, a model of the hillside where the landslide happened, and the judge has ruled that we will take a bus out to the site for a jury view. Do you think there might be a better trial for you to sit on as a juror?"

He said, "No, not at all."

I asked, "Well how do you plan to receive this evidence that will require the ability to see it?"

He said, "I assume the lawyers will describe it accurately."

After thirty years of trial work, I can say a few things with certainty and one of those is that it is very unlikely a lawyer is going to describe the visual evidence accurately. We see only what we want to see, and very often our role as advocate slants what we see.

In my state a statute says the qualifications of a juror include the sensory organs necessary to the task. I made a challenge for cause on account of the juror's lack of eyesight. Plaintiff's attorney objected on the grounds of the Americans with Disabilities Act, which requires government and businesses to accommodate persons with disabilities. He argued that jurors are temporary employees of the county and the ADA requires employers to accommodate persons with a disability like blindness. After hearing argument the judge, obviously a bit aggravated with the lawyer who asked for this ruling, granted my challenge and excused the juror.

ᚠ ᚠ ᚠ

I always try to use the *voir dire* process to introduce the jury to what will come when we start presenting the evidence. It builds a little trust when what you say is going to happen does happen. The blind juror allowed me to let the rest of them know there would be photographs, drawings, a model and a field trip.

In that same case, one of the prospective jurors was an editor of the Seattle Post Intelligencer; at that time it was our morning newspaper, known as the PI. The case arose during a Thanksgiving weekend storm when heavy rain caused the landslide that was at issue in the case. I figured the newspaper editor was probably a reporter that weekend and, in the guise of finding out if he could be a fair and impartial juror of the facts of the case, I asked him to describe what he knew about the rain, the landslides and the havoc in the region all of which gave context to our defense of the case. My client, a grizzled old drilling and retaining wall contractor with one lung, was not a fan of the Post Intelligencer, and on our next break he shuffled up to me and said so all could hear, "I don't know what you are doing with all these chummy questions, but you better get rid of that guy from the fucking P-I." I did as I was told.

人　人　人

In a military trial an enlisted man has a right to a jury consisting one third of enlisted personnel. A vote of two thirds of the jury is required to convict. The enlisted jury pool at the boot camp consisted mostly of current and former drill instructors, and they were not inclined to lightly vote "guilty." With one third of the jury as former drill instructors, if you worked your preemptory challenge just right, you'd get a jury in which the vote of at least one of the former drill instructors was necessary to convict. Getting a conviction was especially difficult when the drill instructor was accused of calling a recruit a name like "sissy." In those days, that was literally a Federal crime. This was my introduction to *jury nullification*.

Jury nullification occurs when the jury is allowed to or believes they have the right to judge the justice of the case, in addition to deciding whether the prosecution has proven its case beyond a reasonable doubt. For example, when the jury acquits the defendant or favors one side or the other in a case because they find the law or its application under the circumstances of the case to be unjust or too harsh, jury nullification occurs. Our common law history includes many examples of jury nullification.

In *Georgia vs. Brailsford*, 3 U.S. 1 (1794), the first Chief Justice of the U.S. Supreme Court, John Jay, wrote: "It is presumed, that juries are the best judges of facts; it is, on the other hand, presumed that courts are the best judges of law. But still both objects are within your power of decision . . . you have a right to take it upon yourselves to judge both, and to determine the law as well as the fact in controversy." In merry old England, theft of more than twenty shillings was a capital offense, and more than once a jury acquitted a defendant who stole more than twenty shillings but did so in order to feed his family. In New England before the Civil War it was common for juries to acquit those who harbored run-away slaves. More recently, jury nullification occurs with low-level marijuana possession cases.

Judges usually hate jury nullification. They see themselves as the law in that courtroom and often act as though "nobody, by God, better ignore my commandments." Under the UCMJ, all jurors take an oath by which they swear to faithfully and impartially try the case, "according to the evidence, your conscience, and the laws applicable to trials by courts-martial." The first time I incorporated this language and asked the jury to use "your conscience" in my closing argument on behalf of a drill instructor who was charged with a crime for calling a recruit by a name other than "recruit" or "private," the judge cut me off mid sentence.

He admonished the jury: "That is what it [the oath] says but that is not what you will do. You will apply the law to this case."

Using my peremptory challenge carefully, I won my first few cases as a defense lawyer and came to believe it had something to do with my confident Louis Nizer-like oratory.

ㅅ ㅅ ㅅ

In the case of Sergeant Rusty (I changed his name), we narrowly avoided complete disaster, and the lesson I learned is to sometimes be wary of what your client tells you. Sergeant Rusty was charged with six counts of theft for stealing wallets from the foot lockers of the recruits in his charge. Thievery is one of the worst offenses in the military because personal privacy is rare and trust among your platoon mates is very important. The charges of theft caused emotions on the base to run high.

I sent Sgt. Rusty out for a polygraph examination. According to the report, his denial was truthful. Polygraph results then and now generally are not admissible unless the prosecution consents; the science has not caught up with the popular notion that the lie detector can detect the liar. But I tried to put it into evidence anyway, and the judge conducted an extensive hearing out of the presence of the jury, ultimately ruling that the evidence was not admissible.

During trial, we called in two character witnesses: the Director of the Drill Instructor School, who was a highly decorated thirty-year Marine Corps veteran, and the priest from Sgt. Rusty's church, who testified about his honesty and care when handling the Sunday service collection basket. Sgt. Rusty also testified.

The evidence in support of five of the charges was strong but Sgt. Rusty wanted to deny the allegations. The evidence in support of the sixth charge was nearly non-existent. Just before Sgt. Rusty took the stand, I asked for a hearing out the presence of the jury in order to make a *motion in limine*. A motion in limine is a process by which the trial lawyer can prevent the introduction of evidence or issues that may be harmful to the case. Under the rules of evidence, otherwise relevant evidence can be excluded if it might be unfairly prejudicial or inflammatory. Ordinarily it is best to make your motions *in limine* before the trial begins, but you should keep your eye out for the chance to use it during trial. In this case, the right to remain silent was at issue.

Right before my client took the stand, out of the presence of the jury, I told the judge and prosecutor that Sergeant Rusty was going to testify about the first five charges, but he was going to exercise his right to remain silent as to the sixth charge. I said I didn't want the prosecutor to "accidentally" blunder into testimony about the sixth charge in his cross examination and force me to object in front of the jury. The prosecutor made no serious objection to my request, and the judge granted my motion.

The jury deliberated for several hours and returned a verdict of guilty on all but the sixth charge.

In the military system, the trial moves immediately into the sentencing phase. I argued extensively about the three potential purposes of punishment; these are deterrence, rehabilitation, and vengeance and I made an impassioned plea to leave vengeance to God. After deliberating several more hours, the jury rendered its sentence late on Friday afternoon: a reduction in rank to Private and sixty days in the brig. The jury decided that a bad conduct discharge was not warranted. This came as quite a shock to all the officers on base, some of whom told me at the Officers' Club later that night that they hated me for what I had done.

To give Sgt. Rusty time to get his affairs in order, I asked the convening authority, who brings the charges, to grant Sgt. Rusty until Monday morning to report to the brig. My request was granted. Later that day, after reporting to the brig, his superior NCO opened up Sgt. Rusty's locker to draw up an inventory of his personal possessions and he found the wallets of the six recruits who had testified at the court martial. Nobody was more surprised than me.

⋏ ⋏ ⋏

In addition to training recruits, the San Diego boot camp is the headquarters command for all recruiting efforts west of the Mississippi River. In 1982 a scandal erupted in the recruiting station at Portland, Oregon. After a lengthy investigation, six recruiters were charged with crimes. The boss came to my office and said, "Mike, I'd like you to handle these cases."

Recruiting young men and women to join the Marines was not easy work in those days. Civilian jobs were more available then and only a unique personality would be attracted to a sales pitch that advertised you would go to interesting places, meet interesting people, and kill them. The recruiters had quotas to fill, and they worked independently, typically at high schools and gyms within their territories. At the Portland office many recruiters became extra creative in the quest to fulfill their recruiting quotas. They found a way to manufacture high school transcripts and driver's licenses for those marginal kids who lacked adequate documentation. With some help from the forgers, the Portland office consistently met or exceeded its quotas for new recruits.

The problem was that these were fraudulent enlistments. Consequently, if the recruits were charged with a crime under the UCMJ, a court martial would have no jurisdiction over them. Most of these kids made it through boot camp and went on to serve without any problems, but a few did not. When several of these cases surfaced in boot camp, the creative shenanigans in the Portland recruiting station unraveled.

I received orders to relocate to Portland, where the prosecutor and I took rooms at a Marriott hotel for six weeks while we dealt with these cases. The Convening Authority who signed the charges was in San Francisco. I realized that I might have to deal with him after I figured out who my clients were and what their story was, so I arranged to meet him in San Francisco. My thinking paid off. In one of the cases, I was able to persuade him to reduce the crime to a non-judicial punishment, which meant no jail time or reduction in rank would be imposed. Word got back to me that he was not happy the prosecutor did not show the Convening Authority the same courtesy.

After the trials began, the prosecutor, the judge, and I would retire to a Portland bar for drinks. We were careful not to talk about the cases, and it was a good time to get to know the judge a little better.

The judge asked me "Mike, what are you planning to do when you get out?"

I said, "I like this criminal law work and I think I'll stick with it when I leave the Marine Corps."

He said, "My advice is to avoid criminal defense work. I believe if you have criminals for clients long enough, you will become one."

⅄ ⅄ ⅄

The judge was concerned about how we would find a jury if the defendants wanted a jury trial. We were not at a military base and it was unclear if we would use local reservists or have to bring in jurors from San Diego. He suggested it might be okay if we tried the cases to the bench with no jury. I was young and impressionable and agreed. It was a wise decision because the sentences were very light. Once later a judge talked me out of a jury and I will never let that happen again.

Not long after we moved to Seattle, I tried a case for a realtor who was sued by the buyer of property the realtor owned. The buyer claimed the septic system drain field was failing when they bought the property and the seller knew it and concealed this information. Plaintiff sued for fraud, breach of contract and negligence. The case was pending in Clallam County on the northern tip of the Olympic Peninsula, and a visiting judge from Jefferson County came in to try the case. During a conference in chambers before the trial began, with a wink and a nod, the judge lead me to believe the fraud case could not be proven, and maybe it would be best if we waived a jury trial. We waived the jury and he went on to find that fraud, breach of contract, and negligence was proven and he awarded substantial damages. That was a bad mistake and one I won't repeat. My client's insurance did not cover fraud, they never do. Fortunately, the insurer paid to settle the case.

⅄ ⅄ ⅄

After the recruiter cases were finished, the boss moved me over to the prosecution. In my last year of service in the Marines I had the job of prosecutor played by Kevin Bacon in the movie *A Few Good Men*, and I had a case similar to the one portrayed in the movie. This case taught me the importance of the appearance of justice.

In *United States v. Sergeant Peters* (I changed his name), a platoon drill instructor was charged with battery at a General Court Martial. He had ordered two of his recruits to "straighten out" another recruit who wasn't catching on to the routine of boot camp as fast as the others. It was against the rules to bring food back from the mess hall, and the DI caught the recruit with chocolate cake from the mess hall in his foot locker. One of the enforcers was a Golden Gloves boxer, and he punched the chocolate cake lover once in the belly, and the blow ruptured the recruit's spleen. Later that day he passed out in the swimming pool and was transported to the Balboa Naval Hospital. The doctors couldn't figure out what might be wrong with the kid, and the emergency room doctor on duty leaned in close to speak to him and learned what happened.

During the trial the doctor testified, "I said to him, son, you are very ill and we need to know what happened. I know sometimes things happen in boot camp that are not supposed to happen, but if you don't tell us what happened, then I believe you are going to die."

The young man told the doctor the story about getting punched and that enabled them to do the test to find the ruptured spleen. He lived, but he lost his spleen and this was a serious problem. It had the attention of the commanding officers all the way to the top. Although a senior officer did not commit suicide as was the case in *A Few Good Men*, the Marine Corps Commandant paid us a visit the day before the trial began and he spoke to all the officers and noncommissioned officers about recruit abuse. General Barrow, a four-star general, was not a Colonel Jessup/Jack Nicholson character. But he was the most senior officer in the Marine Corps and he was speaking to what was, not coincidentally, the jury pool.

General Barrow had enlisted in the Marine Corps right out of high school and he went to boot camp at Parris Island. On this sunny San Diego day, he spoke about recruit abuse in his day, which consisted of nothing worse than the drill instructor dumping a poorly packed foot locker on the floor. He said a drill instructor who abuses a recruit is disloyal because all drill instructors are subject to orders that prohibit abuse. He is stupid because he will be caught. He is a coward because the recruit cannot defend himself. And a drill instructor that uses other recruits to abuse a fellow recruit is a super coward. The Commandant said he wanted nobody of that ilk in his Marine Corps. The general's admonitions were probably unnecessary because the command had stacked the jury to ensure there were no former drill instructors in the venire. All the enlisted members came from the band.

Under the UCMJ it is a crime called "unlawful command influence" for a commanding officer to seek to influence the decisions of a jury. The defense attorneys immediately filed motions seeking a dismissal of the charges or change of venue. They argued, not unreasonably, that General Barrow had tainted the entire jury pool.

As the prosecutor assigned to try the case, it was not a good time for me to take a Gandhi-like principled stand against injustice, and I made what arguments I could. There was no dispute that a crime was committed. Before the trial judge denied all the motions, he allowed individual *voir dire*, and we brought each of the prospective jurors in for questioning about what appeared to be unlawful command influence.

Every one of them said: "Yes, Sir, I was there and I recall General Barrow told us about drill instructors who were disloyal stupid cowards, and I especially recall that he said a drill instructor who used a recruit to abuse another recruit was a super-coward and how he wanted none of those in his Marine Corps".

And every one of them said, "No, Sir, it will have no impact on my decision here."

Sergeant Peters, in fact, had committed a serious crime. Like the desperado in our criminal law casebook who recklessly shot at a passing train and killed a passenger, he set in motion a force likely to commit grievous bodily injury. But Sgt. Peters was no desperado. The opposite was true, and he took the stand and testified all about what was a serious error of judgment. He was convicted of battery, reduced in rank to Private, dishonorably discharged and sentenced to a year in prison at the federal penitentiary at Fort Leavenworth.

It's not a victory that makes me proud. It taught me that the appearance of justice can be as important as the outcome.

Chapter 2

A Product Liability

"There is a right way, a wrong way, and the Navy way," said the retired Navy Chief on the second day of jury selection in the case brought by The Estate of Perry McDonald. The McDonald case was the first asbestos case to be tried in Kitsap County, where the Puget Sound Naval Shipyard was the largest employer. I could not have hired a better witness for what we were about to show the jury, as soon as it was seated.

⅄ ⅄ ⅄

My contract with the Marines was up in May 1982, and I found work with a defense firm in Seattle that June. Two of my law school drinking buddies, one of them a former Marine, worked at the law firm now known as "Lee Smart," and they told me the firm was hiring. The law firm represented Owens Corning Fiberglass, which was one of fifteen or so manufacturers that were sued in those days and a major player in the asbestos litigation, and the firm needed experienced trial lawyers to handle the trials. Over six hundred asbestos product liability suits were pending and the trials were about to begin.

The litigation was spawned by an epidemic of illnesses caused by the inhalation of asbestos at work places all over the country. Before it began to erupt in the late 1970's, the epidemic brewed for decades in the bodies of the men who worked in the shipyards and refineries and those of the wives and mothers who washed their work clothes. Asbestos was used in insulations applied to steam pipes and boilers; and hundreds of millions of feet of these materials were used in industrial refineries, paper mills, and office buildings throughout Western Washington, and in every U.S. Navy ship and shipyard in Seattle, Bremerton, Tacoma and Swan Island north of Portland, Oregon. At a Kaiser shipyard in Portland at one point during the Second World War they produced a new baby flat-top aircraft carrier every day.

Asbestos is a mineral that has been dug from the ground for thousands of years. During the nineteenth century, asbestos became increasingly popular among builders and manufacturers, due to its fireproofing and insulation qualities, as well as its affordability. Despite a few documented cases that came to light, the health risks associated with asbestos production and products were largely ignored. Asbestos filled the air in the holds of the ships where the pipefitters, welders, insulators and a dozen other trades worked. The men drew it into their lungs with every breath, and the mineral scarred the tissue where the lungs exchange air with the body's blood stream.

It is not a poison that makes you sick right away and the effects of asbestos are not reversible. Heavy doses resulted in the scarring known as *asbestosis* ten or fifteen years later while smaller doses led to lung cancer twenty or so years later, especially among smokers. Minute doses could lead to *mesothelioma*, a particularly virulent cancer of the lining of the cavity that contains the lungs or abdomen or the heart, often forty or more years later.

Asbestos claims are the longest running mass tort in U.S. history. Over 4,500,000 men and women worked in the naval shipyards during the Second World War. According to a Rand report, by the time I arrived in Seattle in 1982, over 21,000 product liability suits for asbestos-related illnesses had been filed nationally. Puget Sound had many shipyards at one time;

eventually thousands of claims were filed in our state and federal courts, and our firm's first trials were about to begin.

⋏ ⋏ ⋏

My timing was not very good. Two months after I was hired, Johns Manville, the largest manufacturer and supplier of asbestos-containing products, declared bankruptcy, and the litigation ground to a halt. Under U.S. bankruptcy law, an automatic stay of proceedings is imposed upon the filing of the petition in bankruptcy. Every one of those companies in the McDonald case eventually ended up in bankruptcy, and over sixty more would be added during the next twenty years. Nobody knew what to do when Manville filed its bankruptcy petition. The local presiding judges entered a six-month stay of all the cases, and the pending trials were postponed.

Sensing my concern, the partners at the law firm assured me that my job was safe.

⋏ ⋏ ⋏

While I was working as a Marine Corps Judge Advocate, I was in court frequently with high profile cases and plenty of action, but now it seemed I might never see the inside of a courtroom again for a long time. One day Fred Smart, one of our senior partners, came down the hall and asked if I could cover a motion for him that morning. I jumped at the chance to get back into court. Fred explained that the issue was a settled area of law and I could learn what I needed to know by reading the motion papers on my way to the courthouse. Recalling those bail hearings after lunch with Steve Ray at El Toro Marine Base, I thought, "No problem."

In Mr. Smart's case, we represented a plaintiff named Fred Dore, who had leased some property he owned. The suit sought rescission of the lease because it had not been properly acknowledged. Mr. Smart had filed a jury demand and the defendant lessee filed a motion to strike the jury demand. As far as I could tell, the issue was whether or not we were entitled to a jury trial. In my asbestos work up to that point, we filed and argued Civil Rule 56 motions for summary judgment, and I had learned that a motion for summary judgment could be defeated by showing there were genuine issues of material fact that only a jury should decide.

So when it came time to argue against the motion to strike our jury demand, I told the judge, "Your honor, there are issues of fact that the jury should decide."

The judge said, "Oh yeah, Mr. Bond, like what?"

Not knowing much about the client or the case, I made up something, and my argument failed. The judge granted the motion to strike the jury demand.

When I got back to the office, I walked into Mr. Smart's office with my tail between my legs to deliver the bad news. After telling him I had lost, I said, "By the way Fred, why did you want a jury in this case?"

He said, "Our client is the Chief Justice of the Washington Supreme Court, and I thought the trial judge might be more comfortable if a jury decided the case." I remember thinking, "Oh, *that* Mr. Dore!"

⅄ ⅄ ⅄

The six-month stay of the asbestos cases gave me more time to learn who my client was and the facts of these cases. As there were too many cases for one firm to work them all up, the suits were divided among all the law firms in Seattle and Tacoma, with a lead counsel firm for each case. Lead counsel was responsible to gather the records, take the necessary pretrial depositions, retain the experts, and prepare the case for settlement or trial. Our firm was lead counsel for the McDonald case. As my good fortune would have it, the case was assigned to me. The retired Navy chief's welcome observation during jury selection that "there was a right way, a wrong way, and a Navy way" was the first of many helpful surprises during the trial.

We had two months of pretrial hearings in which Judge James Maddock reviewed all of the out-of-state depositions and the trial exhibits that were going to be used at trial. Six large manufacturers remained in the case and the plaintiff's attorneys gave us notice that they intended to use dozens of depositions and thousands of pages of exhibits. As lead counsel, I was primarily responsible to attend these hearings to argue the admissibility of all this evidence. The extensive pretrial process to review the evidence to be offered at trial proved to be very useful when the trial got underway.

As lead counsel for this first case, the extensive pretrial hearing also allowed me to set the course of the trial to come. I like having that control over the details. Usually with many parties on one side or the other, every lawyer wants to run the show. You run the risk that the outcome will resemble a camel which, the old saying goes, is a horse designed by a committee. I usually do my own appeals too. In fact, when I am drafting the answer to the complaint, often I begin thinking about the discovery to come, the trial and the possible appeal, all of which will depend on the record you make in the trial court.

Approximately two weeks before the trial began, we took the deposition of the widow, Mrs. McDonald. The McDonalds had a long and happy marriage, and she had been a witness to the devastating impact asbestos allegedly had on her husband's health. She was entitled to damages for the loss of her husband,

and we needed to know what she was going to say and how she might come across with the jury.

⅄ ⅄ ⅄

A jury trial rarely has much to do with a search for the truth. During one of my Marine Corps trials, I kept exclaiming to the judge, "Your honor, my client is innocent." After I said that the second or third time, the judge thundered back at me, like Moses scolding a nonbeliever: "Counsel, no man is innocent! That is not the issue. In this trial the issue is can the government prove its case beyond a reasonable doubt?" A trial is less about truth than it is about the evidence that is marshaled to prove the case.

The rules of evidence and procedure are often designed to prevent the jury from hearing or seeing all the truth about a case. During the two months of pretrial hearings in the *McDonald* case, we argued about every evidentiary rule in the book. Some parts of the evidence either side wanted to use was to be excluded or subject to a limiting instruction, meaning the judge would tell the jury it would be admitted but only for a limited purpose.

Because the truth may not be relevant, or may be unfairly prejudicial, or hard to find, in my experience what does seems to matter most is how the plaintiff or defendant comes across. How will the jury react to them? It's useful to consider several questions, including

- Are these nice people or not?
- Is their cause just or do they seek something else?
- Are they worthy in some intangible way or not?

⅄ ⅄ ⅄

Mrs. McDonald and her lawyers came to my office for the deposition. We were in a small conference room, and all the seats were filled with lawyers and paralegals for the six defendants still in the case. We knew from the medical records that Mr. McDonald had been taking pure oxygen by a mask in his later years, and increasing quantities of oxygen did not seem to help. He slowly suffocated to death — literally. Toward the end of the deposition, I asked Mrs. McDonald if she believed her husband experienced any pain or suffering during the last six months of his life.

The conference room was silent. Tension was in the air. Her husband had died more than two years ago, and Mrs. McDonald looked at me for a moment or two when she burst into gasping, wailing, sobs of grief. She cried as I have never before or since seen a woman cry, and I've seen too many women cry.

I believe she had not grieved the loss of her husband before that moment. He died a slow miserable death before her eyes, and no doubt it was an awful thing. But before she had any reason to talk about it, she busied herself arranging a funeral, taking care of the estate, finding a lawyer, and figuring out what she would do with the rest of her life. I reached this conclusion because at trial she was as cold as ice and showed very little emotion, and I'm sure that made it easier for the jury to decide she would receive no award.

⅄ ⅄ ⅄

Among the various types of damages sought in these cases, the estate made a claim for the loss of earnings on account of his disability. Mr. McDonald retired from the shipyard and he claimed he had to retire on account of asbestosis. A few days before the trial began, the defense economist, Vince Jolivet, brought it to my attention that the income tax returns showed Mr. McDonald collected unemployment compensation in the last few years of his life after leaving the shipyard. He said, "You should look into this because I believe the law says you cannot claim unemployment unless you represent that you are ready, able and willing to work." Obviously, that would not be consistent with a claim for disabling lung disease.

During my opening statement to the jury, I mentioned only that there was some "funny business" about unemployment compensation shown in the income tax returns. I left it hanging in the air, like a bright piñata full of candy, and Mrs. McDonald's lawyers rose to swing at it with all their might.

While presenting Mrs. McDonald's direct testimony, her lawyer, Paul Whelan, retrieved a document from his breast pocket. He reminded her that I had said something about "funny business" and unemployment, and he handed the document to the clerk so it could be marked as an exhibit. When I asked the judge if I could see it, he wanted to know if it was previously produced. I assured him that we had not seen it until that moment.

The document was an order from the unemployment office declaring that Mr. McDonald's departure from the shipyard was not a voluntary quit. Workers who voluntarily quit are not entitled to unemployment compensation. It turned out that Mr. McDonald filed for unemployment after he left the shipyard, but some clerk ruled that it was a voluntary quit and so he cut off the benefits, and Mr. McDonald appealed the clerk's decision. On appeal, the clerk's decision to cut off the unemployment was reversed. Mrs. McDonald's lawyers simply wanted to show there was no funny business about it.

In protest I reminded Judge Maddock that we had spent two full months, five days a week, reviewing the evidence that was going to be offered, and yet this document from the unemployment office had not been produced or disclosed to us as it should have been. I added, "and Judge, this order must have come from a file, and we would like to see the rest of the file before there is any more testimony about it."

Judge Maddock ordered production of the file, and we obtained it the next day. Among other interesting things, the file contained a three-page handwritten statement, made under oath, in which Mr. McDonald said he had a disability on account of a back injury that prevented him from climbing ladders. His statement said he had a little shortness of breath, but it did not slow him down, and he claimed he never went to doctors because it was against his religion. That statement about never going to see doctors, under oath no less, was not true.

When Mrs. McDonald returned to testify, I cross-examined her about her husband's statement. She identified her husband's handwriting and signature, and I asked her to read to the jury what he said, as if he was calling from his grave.

人 人 人

The medical case was not simple and, contrary to his sworn denial about seeing doctors, Mr. McDonald had been examined by many specialists. His doctors had considerable difficulty making a diagnosis and several possibilities were explored before they settled on asbestosis. The chest x-rays appeared normal and the pulmonary function tests made little sense, which explained why it had been so difficult to make a diagnosis. Our pulmonary medical expert, Dr. Dorsett Smith, suggested using the pulmonary function tests to prove his conclusion that Mr. McDonald had a congenital defect that reduced the blood flow to his lungs. He concluded that condition and not asbestosis caused Mr. McDonald to be short of breath.

I allowed Dr. Smith to choose the pulmonary function tests he would use to support his diagnosis. One test was not like the others, but he told me to leave it out of his testimony and I did not know better. Now I do. On cross-examination, Mrs. McDonald's lawyer was able to raise doubt about Dr. Dorsett's conclusion with the one test result we did not discuss. It would have been better if I had used it in my direct examination, and then explained why it was of no consequence. That way the jury would know about it and it wouldn't look like we were trying to hide it. The lesson I learned is that the lawyer should always decide what evidence to offer. Don't leave it up to the expert.

ᚼ ᚼ ᚼ

Dr. Corwin Hinshaw was a lung disease specialist from San Francisco and one of our expert witnesses. He was eighty-two years old by this time and had testified in hundreds of asbestos cases. He developed the iron lung for polio victims; he helped find the cure for tuberculosis; and he wrote the leading medical school textbook on lung disease. He was a vain man who wore makeup to conceal his age, and he had a terrific manner on the witness stand. After answering the lawyer's questions in precise medical terminology, he would turn to the jury and say in a Marcus Welby, MD manner, "And the point is, this man does not have any of the criteria necessary for a diagnosis of asbestosis."

Dr. Hinshaw was on the witness stand for most of the day and his testimony was concluded by mid-afternoon. We were in about the fifth or sixth week of trial and, sensing everybody in the courtroom was out of steam, Judge Maddock said we would take the rest of the afternoon off. The bailiff escorted the jury to the jury room and she returned a few minutes later to say, "The jury wants to know, if they buy a copy of Dr. Hinshaw's book will he sign it?" That was a good sign.

ᴧ ᴧ ᴧ

These were product liability lawsuits and, roughly speaking, a manufacturer would be liable for a defective product if it was proven to be dangerous to an extent not anticipated by the ordinary user of the product, or if the manufacturer was negligent in the design of the product, or in failing to warn consumers how to use the product safely. Liability turned on what the ordinary users knew about the hazards of the product. We learned in discovery that Shop 56 in the Naval Shipyard at Bremerton had published a manual of procedures for the pipefitters and insulators. It seemed to me that these were the ordinary users of the asbestos-containing materials used in the shipyard, and if these men knew of the risk of lung disease from unsafe asbestos work practices, then we might argue the products were reasonably safe and therefore not defective. The product liability law in our state and most states says there is no duty to warn when the hazards are known or obvious.

A very nice fellow named Burt Workman helped draft the *Shop 56 Manual*, and we called him in to testify about it. *The Shop 56 Manual* was an admitted exhibit, one of the hundreds we reviewed during the two months of pretrial hearings. I had my staff prepare a copy of several helpful pages from the manual, and the clerk distributed a set to each of the jurors so they could read along with Mr. Workman as I asked questions about it.

I use this technique whenever I can. Some trial lawyers have grown used to using a screen with a projected image of the exhibit, often stored in a laptop or on a thumb drive, and that is one way to present the evidence. I believe the evidence is more likely to be read and recalled later when the jurors have it in their hands and can see for themselves that you have not taken the message out of context or misused it some way. Projected images can be manipulated, and they are usually shown only so briefly that the information does not sink in as well as when the juror can physically hold it and read what he or she wants. Save the projected image for use in your closing argument; it will remind the jury of what they once held in their hands.

As Mr. Workman and I worked our way through the *Shop 56 Manual*, he began to project pride in his work. He had researched the issue of asbestos and found a story about Charlemagne, who would throw a tablecloth into the fire and it would come out clean because it was a textile made entirely from asbestos. He wrote that the old-timers knew of "miners pthosis," which he said was a lung disease caused by asbestos, and that some of the old timers would speak sardonically about using respirators when working with or around asbestos.

I reached under the podium I was using for my questioning and retrieved a dictionary and said,

"Mr. Workman, I make my living with words, and I had a bit of trouble with that word "sardonically" in this context. It says here it refers to scorn or mockery or satire. Why would the old timers speak satirically about using respirators to prevent lung disease?"

He replied, "I don't know, who knows why people do what they do; look at the Green River killer." I paused to think about that one.

The Green River killer was a serial murderer of women on the loose in Western Washington; about twenty-five years later he was arrested, and in exchange for avoiding the death penalty, he lead the Sheriff's investigators to the locations of over fifty women he had slain. Only ten or twenty had disappeared when

Mr. Workman brought it into our trial. It was too bizarre to say anything more.

⋏ ⋏ ⋏

After two months of trial, our closing arguments took more than two full days starting on June 7, which happened to be the fortieth Anniversary of the D-Day landing in World War II. Elderly Veterans from the VFW were at the courthouse doors handing out poppies. A lawyer from the plaintiff's law firm, Michael Withey, came to watch and coincidentally he sat beside my wife, who also came to watch the arguments. He was wearing a purple corduroy suit, and I guess he thought she might think that was special. She's a very friendly woman, and after a bit of chit chat with him, she let him know she was my wife. He moved quickly to another seat.

After ten weeks of trial and two and half days of final argument, the jury started deliberations at 3:00 p.m. on a Friday afternoon. They told us later that the first vote right away was ten to two for the defense, but they wanted to give it the weekend so it didn't look so bad. They returned a verdict for the defense Monday afternoon. In speaking to the jury afterward, one young woman said, "We figured if Mr. McDonald had fought in the war, he would have died a long time ago."

After thirty years of jury cases, I rarely talk to the jurors any more when it is over. In federal court speaking with the jurors after the trial is prohibited by rule. Many times one or more of the jurors would ask for my business card, which is flattering. But too many times I found that they decide cases for really odd reasons. Sometimes they make the right decision for the right reasons, sometimes they make the right decision for the wrong reasons, and sometimes they make the wrong decision for God only knows what reasons. As the saying goes, ignorance is bliss, and I prefer to remain happy.

⅄ ⅄ ⅄

The first 600 asbestos cases in our office usually consisted of legitimate claims for injury. In some we had valid defenses, which included the impact of smoking on the development of lung cancer, the expiration of a statute of limitations, or how to allocate causation among dozens of potentially liable manufacturers.

The litigation was massive, thousands of new cases were filed every year, and while the company's insurance held out, the claims were tried or settled. All of the large companies that were sued in the early years eventually entered bankruptcy. Many entrepreneurial lawyers all over the country took up the cause of the injured workers, some of whom were not injured at all. It was and still is a gravy train of easy money. Late night television ads solicit claims by telling viewers that billions of dollars in bankruptcy trusts are there for the taking.

One technique the entrepreneurs used was to conduct massive screening programs in which the workers, who were identified by their union affiliation, were invited to a screening to determine if they had an asbestos disease for which compensation might be due. And one such screening program lead to over 200 suits filed in 2004 on behalf of former aluminum workers at an Alcoa Aluminum Company smelter in Wenatchee, Washington.

⅄ ⅄ ⅄

I was retained to defend one defendant that supplied products used in the smelter process to control the flow of molten aluminum. The company had never been sued before because their products did not contain asbestos. We were unable to convince any of the judges to dismiss our client because the plaintiff's lawyers were able to create an issue of fact that required a jury to decide the case.

Alcoa kept track of its inventory of these molten aluminum flow control products with five by seven inch inventory cards; this was before industry began to use computers and electronic record keeping. The inventory cards showed what was once an asbestos-containing product was replaced by my client's asbestos-free product by the early 1970's. The trouble is, Alcoa didn't start over with new inventory cards, they just added the new products to the old cards. Plaintiffs' experts claimed the inventory cards showed these were all asbestos-containing products, and that testimony overcame my client's own witnesses who said it was not so. So we tee'd up three of the claims for a consolidated trial.

We worked up medical experts who believed none of the workers had any asbestos disease at all. In fact, all of these retired workers were living quit contentedly on their retirement pensions and playing golf in good health as far as they knew when they were invited to the screening. We had industrial hygiene experts who helped us tell the story of how these products were used in the smelter. The founder of the company was a very nice man who was born and raised in New Zealand and passionate about his efforts to develop and market the asbestos-free product. The three retired aluminum workers were as honest as the day is long. And we had several nice surprises during trial.

ᴧ ᴧ ᴧ

In my opening statement to the jury, I presented the facts of the cases and said, "You will see that not one of these men is, in fact, sick with any illness, let alone an asbestos disease." As it happened, I had to correct that bold assertion when we came to closing arguments.

Each of the bankrupt companies established trusts to administer the claims against them, and the law firms who pursue these cases are adept at submitting claim forms to the trusts to obtain compensation for their clients, usually at a scheduled rate depending on the disease. A case of mesothelioma in a relatively young person gets the most; those with non-disabling scarring usually get the least. In our county, plaintiffs are required before trial to disclose to the defendants what settlements they have obtained, including the bankruptcy trust payments. This enables the remaining defendants to seek an offset against what they might have to pay.

The three retired aluminum workers in our trial case gave us notice of the settlements. We were surprised to learn that one of the workers received a settlement from Kaiser Aluminum, which operated a smelter in Tacoma, Washington. This meant that he had not fully disclosed to us in discovery the extent of his prior employment, which would most likely include exposures to other asbestos-containing products. Maybe his alleged illness had been caused by one of those other companies.

During my cross-examination of this gentleman, I planned to set up his failure to disclose this other employment or his possible exposures to other asbestos-containing products in an effort to impeach his credibility, and I handed him the notice of settlement his lawyers had given us. When plaintiff's counsel, who was with a California law firm, objected to my question, I asked for a side bar conference with the judge out of the presence of the jury. In chambers I told the judge that there was something fishy about the plaintiff's case because this information about the worker's employment at Kaiser was not disclosed in his responses to interrogatories about former employers. The judge was not too happy that this was such a surprise in view of the case-handling orders that were intended to prevent just such surprises from happening and what appeared to be incomplete or inaccurate discovery responses. I asked her to compel the plaintiff to produce the claim form they had submitted to the bankruptcy court, and she granted my request.

I reported these events to my client's insurers at the end of the day. The next morning one of the adjusters sent me a copy of a lengthy motion filed in an asbestos lawsuit against a tobacco company in Ohio. The motion sought sanctions against this same California law firm for all kinds of transgressions, including manipulation of the claims submitted to various bankruptcy trusts. I had stumbled into something interesting.

When I arrived in court that morning, the plaintiff's attorney gave me the claim forms, which showed claims of exposure to substantial quantities of asbestos-containing products at the Kaiser Aluminum smelter, all of which made the gentleman's testimony in our case suspect. On my way to lunch that day, I put a copy of the motion in the Ohio case that I received that morning on counsel's table, and I told him it would provide some interesting lunchtime reading.

Just before we started up in the afternoon, he asked me where I got the motion, and I politely declined to say. When I returned to my office that evening after we recessed, a letter was waiting for me. It started out, "Dear Mr. Bond, We represent the California law firm. We understand you are in possession of pleadings filed in Ohio and we want to know where you obtained them . . ." I sent the writer a short email declining his request in colorful terms. Two days later, the front page of the *Wall Street Journal* published a long article all about the Ohio litigation, and I never heard from them again about it. The *Wall Street Journal* was useful in another case several years later.

⋏ ⋏ ⋏

The trial went from bad to worse for the plaintiffs.

All of the workers were good men, honest to a fault, and ready to tell the jury their stories. My cross-examination of Mr. Hart produced an unexpected gem.

I said, "You were notified by your union about a screening for asbestos disease. Is that correct?"

He said, "Yes".

I asked, "Did you go to a doctor's office for the screening?"

"No, we were told to go to the hotel."

I asked, "Were there doctors at the hotel?"

He said, "Yes, and they had lawyers, too."

"Oh, where did the lawyers work, right there in Wenatchee?" I had a feeling that would be unlikely.

"No, I think they were from Texas."

"Did the doctors have their own x-ray machines?"

"Yes, I think the doctor was an osteopath from Illinois"

"Did you meet with the lawyers before you saw the doctors and got your x-rays?"

"Yes."

"What did the lawyers tell you?" Ordinarily that question would draw an objection, but none came.

"I don't really recall."

"And then after you saw the lawyers you went in to see the doctor?"

"Yes."

"Mr. Hart, did you have any idea what they were looking for?"

"Well, yes, I do have an idea." It seemed he wanted to tell me something.

"What do you think they were looking for?"

"I think they were looking for lawsuits!"

I had no idea he was going to say this. It was one of those surprises that will turn the tide in your favor, and I was happy to see all fourteen of our jurors, twelve and two alternates, quickly put their heads down and begin to scribble in the notebooks the court gave them at the beginning of the trial.

λ λ λ

When it came time for closing arguments, I assembled a PowerPoint presentation and I began by apologizing for my assertion in opening statements that none of the men were sick. I was mistaken because we now knew they were suffering from a uniquely American malady. These were the diagnostic criteria for this illness; I put them on the screen one at a time:

- Take one healthy and happy retired aluminum smelter worker,
- Add one Texas lawyer prospecting for lawsuits,
- Add one Illinois osteopath who holds himself out as an M.D. and travels with his own special x-ray machine to local hotels,
- Scare the wits out of the worker by telling him he might get cancer because his x-ray is bad, and
- Tell the worker the lawyer can sue the bastards that did it to him; just sign here.

Put it all together and you will come down with one bad case of: LAWSUIT FEVER.

Only one of the jurors burst out laughing, but I am sure they all were similarly amused. The jury took about thirty minutes to find for the defense in all the cases.

And to avoid a large monetary sanction for discovery abuse, the plaintiffs' law firm agreed to voluntarily dismiss all remaining 200 lawsuits. My partners thought I was crazy to get rid of so many good law suits so easily. Huge legal fees went right out the door. But my clients loved me, and I'll take happy clients over greedy partners any day.

Chapter 3

A Case of Bad Faith

Right after dinner on a cold January evening, Scott Nodel told his parents he was going down to the 7-Eleven store for a few minutes. He obtained his driver's license two weeks earlier as soon as he had turned sixteen. The Nodels lived in Newport Hills and the 7-Eleven was a couple of miles away in Factoria on Richards Road. A new condominium complex was going in at the top of Richards Road, not far from Scott's school, Newport High. Just before he made it to the 7-Eleven, Scott hit a patch of ice and he lost control of the car. It may be he was going a bit fast for the conditions, but I'm sure he didn't see the black ice on the road. The car slid sideways at high speed and wrapped around a telephone pole, causing Scott massive head injuries. As a result, the boy suffered catastrophic brain damage. And that is how the Chaussee case began.

The Nodel family retained Simon Forgette to sue the parties responsible for their son's injuries. As fate would have it, Simon was a Marine Corps Trial Judge when I was with the Marines at San Diego. He left the Marines shortly after I arrived, so I never tried a case in his court. He was a tall, red-haired man, and the guys in San Diego referred to him as the "velvet hammer."

The Nodels first sued King County. They alleged that King County's negligent failure to maintain the roadway or to warn of the ice on the roadway caused the accident that turned Scott Nodel's life into a vegetative tube-fed existence. The boy was unable to move and he could do no more than blink his eyes.

Sometimes they thought he was trying to say something when he blinked.

Not long after filing suit against King County, Simon added a claim against Dean Chaussee and his company. They were the developers of the condominium uphill from Richards Road. The theory was that the construction work at the site altered the flow of rainwater, causing it to flow onto and across the road. There it froze for a day or so before Scott encountered it on the night he drove the family car to the 7-Eleven.

Mr. Chaussee's business was insured with Maryland Casualty Company, a large casualty insurer. As was its usual practice, Maryland Casualty assigned the defense of the case to the Reed McClure law firm in Seattle, and a lawyer I'll call "Frank Duke" got the case.

ﾏ　ﾏ　ﾏ

Under the civil rules governing discovery in cases like this, when the defendants are asked whether they have insurance, they are required to say so and reveal how much insurance they have. A paralegal at the Reed McClure firm called Mr. Chaussee's insurance agent and asked him what insurance Chaussee had. I ended up representing that insurance agent, but I'm getting ahead of my story.

The insurance agent's file clerk told the paralegal that Mr. Chaussee and his company had a general liability policy with $500,000 in limits *and an umbrella policy with $2 million in limits*. This information was true on the date when the paralegal asked the question, but it was not correct as of the date of the accident. The insurance coverage that applied to this claim was the coverage in effect when the accident occurred three years earlier. General liability insurance is based on the date of the incident resulting in the claim. Unlike general liability insurance, professional liability insurance is "claims made," which means the insurance that applies is the insurance in effect when the claim is asserted, at that may be many years after the date of the occurrence. On the date of Scott Nodel's accident, there was no umbrella policy in effect. In fact, there probably was no coverage at all because the condominium project was built by a joint venture that was not named as an insured party under the policy. There was a specific exclusion in such cases, but that issue fell by the wayside.

I don't know why the Reed McClure paralegal called Mr. Chaussee's insurance agent. I always ask the insurance company that hired me to provide the information about coverage. And I always confirm that information in writing with the insurance company's claims representative I'm dealing with. This case proved the wisdom of my usual practice.

The paralegal put the incorrect insurance information into the interrogatory answer, along with additional information about the defendants, the construction project, and potential witnesses. The interrogatories and responses, including the erroneous answer to the question regarding insurance coverage, were delivered to Mr. Forgette's office. The defense lawyers also sent a copy of the responses to the Maryland Casualty adjuster who worked at a regional office in Sacramento, California. The adjuster saw the error in the answer about insurance and he wrote "wrong" in the margin of the answer. He didn't tell anybody there was a mistake. Not long afterward, the adjuster changed jobs. The information lay there in the file, its error unknown to anybody else at the insurance company's Sacramento office or the defense lawyers in Seattle.

⅄ ⅄ ⅄

As the case investigation developed, Mr. Duke periodically reported to the insurance company and Mr. Chaussee that he didn't see a strong basis for liability. To be sure, the injuries were catastrophic. But maybe the boy was speeding and surely the county was to blame. Besides, under Washington law, like all arid Western states, surface water is a "common enemy" and a landowner is not liable if it flows off his property and causes damage.

King County's lawyer was more cautious. He saw the liability potential, and King County settled the Nodel case for payment of $2.5 million.

After completing his settlement with King County, Mr. Forgette asked for a meeting with Mr. Chaussee's legal team. He met in Seattle with the insurance company's local claims manager and Mr. Duke, the defense lawyer, to discuss settlement. After exchanging pleasantries and drinking a little coffee, Simon asked them to pay the insurance policy limits, which he understood were $2.5 million.

I wasn't there but I understand in response to this settlement demand they said something like, "What $2.5 million? The limits are only $500,000."

Simon quickly retrieved his copy of the interrogatory answer and showed it to them. For some odd reason he came prepared on the issue of how much insurance protected Mr. Chaussee and his company. He said something like, "You told me there was $2.5 million in coverage, and I relied on that answer when I negotiated our settlement with King County and my clients released them from any further liability."

The meeting ended very shortly thereafter. This was a problem. The interrogatory answer was incorrect, and the Velvet Hammer with the brain-damaged client said he had relied on the answer when settling with the other defendant. Moving quickly to deal with the problem just a few days after discovering the mistake, Mr. Duke, Mr. Chaussee's defense lawyer, issued a ten-page report to Maryland Casualty. He explained how the Nodel claim was a very certain case of liability with damages that could exceed $7.5 million.

⅄ ⅄ ⅄

Maryland Casualty tendered $500,000 in settlement, but that wasn't going to be enough to make the problem go away. At the end of this stage of the case, the Nodels and Chaussee entered into a settlement agreement for $7.5 million. Mr. Chaussee agreed to entry of a judgment against himself and his company for $7.5 million, with a credit for King County's settlement. And he assigned to the Nodel family his rights to bad faith and negligence against the insurance company, the Reed McClure lawyers, and the insurance agent. In exchange for the assignment of rights, the Nodels executed a covenant not to execute against Mr. Chaussee's assets. This covenant was their promise to limit any further recovery to whatever could be gained from the insurance company, the lawyers and the insurance agent.

In this deal, Nodel and their attorneys were permitted to sue the insurance company, the defense lawyers, and the insurance agent in the name of Mr. Chaussee and his company. Everybody in whom Chaussee had placed his trust had let him down, and their omissions created a large liability for him. What was born as *Nodel vs. King County* grew up to become *Chaussee vs. Maryland Casualty, et al.*

The insurer owes a fiduciary duty to the policy holder. It is one of the highest duties under the law. When an insurance company fails to fulfill its duty to the customer who paid the premium, and damages result, it may be liable to him for bad faith. In this case, it was inexcusable that the regional claims adjuster noted the mistake and said nothing. His file copy with "wrong" written in the margin was a classic smoking gun, a time bomb waiting to explode.

It doesn't matter that Mr. Chaussee didn't have to pay anything. By these assignment of rights deals, one of the lawyers on the case referred to it as a "whorehouse deal", clever lawyers can turn what might be a very tough case on liability with substantial damages – a sow's ear – into a veritable silk purse. What began as a suit against a developer for causing ice to form on the road became a suit against the insurance company, the defense lawyer and the insurance agent for mishandling the defense of the case.

⋏ ⋏ ⋏

Dave Martin, the senior partner at my law firm, came to my office one day after Mr. Forgette filed his new bad faith and negligence suit against the three amigos. Our firm was hired to defend the insurance agent. I had handled several claims against insurance agents by this time.

He said, "Mike, here is a good one to chew on. You can bury a lot of time in the file, if you know what I mean."

I think what he meant was the stakes were high enough, $7.5 million in fact, that the client wouldn't scrutinize our billings too closely. I never did like that approach. I bill what time I spend on a client's business, even if it happens while I'm driving to work. We bill in tenths of an hour, and if I billed a 1.0 that means I spent sixty minutes on the problem, give or take.

These cases against insurance agents were usually very interesting. In the mid 1980's the Alaska King Crab fishery plummeted. I think they overfished the grounds so badly that the authorities in charge of the fishery halted all crabbing for a season or two. Shortly after the King Crab business collapsed, crab boats began sinking all over the North Pacific Ocean. Coincidently, the boats usually went down in water that was thousands of feet deep. Of course, there was no chance of a salvage and not many witnesses either. When the boat owners began to make claims under their marine insurance policies, they found that some of the brokers had placed the coverage with such sturdy sounding companies as the Libyan-Algerian Insurance Company which, of course, couldn't be found to pay the claim. Newspaper reports claimed other brokers didn't buy insurance at all, and instead spent the money on various legal and not so legal recreational pursuits.

In the *Chaussee* case, we had dozens of days of depositions of all the parties: the defense attorneys, the paralegal, insurance representatives, my insurance agent client, and others. And we argued a large number of pretrial motions. The law was not as clear then as it is now that covenant judgments with an assignment of rights are effective. In an assignment of rights with covenant judgment, the main legal issue is whether there are any damages. If the defendant has a judgment against him, but it cannot be collected from his assets, then where is the harm? There is in fact no damage and the defendant will never have to pay anything.

Our courts imagine the harm in order to force insurance companies and their assigned lawyers to be more careful. This approach has a certain logic to it; bad actors should not get away with breaching the fiduciary duty they owe. But I think it is better policy to require disputes to be decided on the merits and not on imagined facts.

人 人 人

As is usually the case everywhere now, but especially in large complex cases, the court set a case schedule for the disclosure of the identity of witnesses, including expert witnesses, and the completion of discovery. When the witness disclosures were filed, we realized that Mr. Forgette intended to call no expert witnesses.

I was expecting to see experts who would testify about the insurance company's claim handling practices, the lawyer's duty of care to the clients, and the insurance agent's duty of care. Lawyers and insurance agents are professionals, and in order to prove they were negligent in the handling of a case, experts usually are called to explain how the professional is supposed to behave and to render opinions that the lawyer or insurance agent failed to exercise proper reasonable care. Insurance companies are not professionals in the same sense, but the rules governing proper claim handling practices are detailed and not something most people know much about. The rules of evidence say that expert opinion is admissible if it will be helpful to the jury.

Instead of calling any experts, Mr. Forgette planned to rely only on the facts of the case. He was going to call each of the witnesses who were involved in the Nodel case, and he figured that they would prove everything that would have to be proven. That was probably good enough for the insurance company because all of the insurance company's representatives agreed that somebody should have corrected the mistake in the interrogatory answer as soon as it was discovered. A failure to follow good industry practices is negligence. But as to a very key set of facts, proving up the case was not going to be so easy.

In a case of bad faith or lawyer negligence, you always have a case-within-a-case. The case against the lawyer is only as strong as the underlying case he messed up. In order to prove the lawyer is liable, you must first show the case, if properly handled, would have had a better result. If the underlying case has no good chance of success anyway, then the malpractice case may not have any value. Most malpractice cases are handled on a contingent fee basis. Plaintiff's counsel in these cases is usually willing to take it on only if the amount of recovery is sufficiently large that the potential of securing a large fee compensates for the risk of losing in the end. The case against the insurance company and insurance agent also was only as strong as the underlying case.

I knew Mr. Forgette would have to introduce evidence of the underlying case – the case of *Nodel vs. Chaussee.* The jurors would have no context for the claims against the insurer, lawyers, and insurance agent unless they learned all about the Nodel case and how it turned out. But rather than call an expert witness to tell the jury what happened and explain why the case was one of clear liability, massive damages, and a case that should have been settled, Mr. Forgette decided to rely only on the testimony of Mr. Duke, the defense lawyer, and his ten-page letter.

I began to look more closely at the letter, which showed a dramatic shift in the evaluation of the case. Up to the day when the mistaken interrogatory was discovered, Mr. Duke was telling the insurance company the case might be winnable. I wondered what had changed to warrant such a dramatic re-evaluation. Were there new facts that had just come to light, or a new court of appeals decision, or some factor other than the discovery of the mistake in the interrogatory? The closer I looked, the more I discovered that the letter was full of fiction. In at least ten instances, the author of the letter referred to evidence that did not exist or he so misrepresented the facts as to call into question the conclusion. I actually found about twenty or so such examples, but we whittled them down to the ten strongest fictions.

Bill Helsell and his firm represented Mr. Duke and his law firm. Helsell was then the dean of the defense trial bar. He was as old as the hills and had tried every case imaginable. Once he testified as an expert witness for a defense firm brought up for sanctions for hiding evidence in a drug product liability case. He testified that it was the lawyer's duty to "duck and dodge" discovery. Now, I think all litigation lawyers should take aggressive stands in the defense of the client. Sometimes an aggressive attack is all you have, but "duck and dodge"? I don't think so, and neither did the Supreme Court when they ruled.

When it became clear that the plaintiff in our case was going to rely exclusively on Mr. Duke's ten-page letter, I met with Helsell and said, "Bill, that is the only evidence they intend to use, and I think it would be a good idea if he would back off that letter."

Helsell would have none of it saying, "Bond, you are fucking crazy. He isn't going to back off that letter."

I tried one more time. "Bill, it's going to be very ugly if he doesn't back off that letter."

"No," he said. He had no idea what was coming.

⋏ ⋏ ⋏

As expected, Plaintiff called Mr. Duke to testify. He identified his role in the case as lawyer for Reed McClure, the law firm Maryland Casualty Company hired to defend Mr. Chaussee and his company. He told of his evaluation of the case and what he did to inform himself about the facts of the case. He identified his ten-page page letter report, and it was admitted into evidence. He said, "those are my opinions. Based on our investigation, the case was one of liability and probable damages that could exceed $7.5 million." The gist of my cross-examination went like this:

First, I had Mr. Duke identify the ten documents or pieces of evidence that he claimed were sources for the statements contained in his report and evaluation. I offered them into evidence and I wrote the name of each one on poster paper on the easel, listing them one through ten in order of the strength of each piece of evidence. Down at number ten, the evidence was weakest and might foster an argument about what it meant.

I said, "Mr. Duke, when you are evaluating a case, you need to form an opinion of how the witnesses will come across, right?"

"Yes."

I remember hearing an appellate advocate at a conference in Hong Kong once say that the answer to the first question in oral argument should always be "no." If you disregard this rule and give them a "yes" to the first question, then you might as well throw the towel in and go home because there is no way back.

I wanted to lay it on thick with the witness. "You are trying to gauge, how will the jury receive this evidence? Will they believe him or not? Right?"

"Yes."

"There are three ways you can evaluate a witness's credibility?"

He said, "I guess so. What do you mean?"

I replied, "Well, you could interview the witness in person, right?

"Yes."

"You could take a deposition of the witness, isn't that true?"

"Yes."

"Or I suppose you could wait until trial to see how the witness performs. Right?"

"I guess you could do that, yes."

Now I set my trap. "What you are looking for are inconsistencies in the witness's testimony, right?"

"Yes, that is right."

"And the more inconsistencies you find, the less likely it is the witness will be believed. Isn't that what you're looking for?"

"Yes, that helps."

"And if you find enough inconsistencies in the witness's testimony, where he said one thing and the evidence shows the opposite is true, if you get enough of those, then the jury may very well conclude that they should not believe a single thing the witness says. Isn't that right?"

I could never have planned what happened next. I had an idea of where I wanted to go and I like to improvise. It forces you to listen carefully to the witness's answer, and this time I hit pay dirt.

Mr. Duke said, "It depends on whether the witness is for you or against you."

I looked at the jury and asked, "Mr. Duke, are you for me or against me?"

He asked me to repeat the question and I looked right at him and repeated my question. I set the hook.

He said, "I am just here to tell the truth."

I said, "Well let's see about that."

I handed him his report and the first piece of evidence listed on the poster. (I don't recall what it was.) I said, "Now, in your report, you said this," and I read it out loud.

He replied, "That is what I said."

"But the exhibit you relied on does not say that at all, does it?"

He refused to answer my question.

I turned to Judge McCutcheon and asked him to instruct the witness to answer the question.

Some trial tactic books say the trial lawyer should never ask the judge for help with a witness because it shows weakness by the examining attorney. I think asking the judge to instruct the witness to answer a question in the middle of trial when used appropriately shows the jury that you are in complete control over what is happening – to the point where the judge does what you asked of him. The trial lawyer who is in command of what happens in the courtroom usually comes out on top. It can be as subtle as keeping an eye on the clock and structuring your examination so you suggest when it would be a good time for the morning or afternoon break.

After the judge ordered him to answer the question, Mr. Duke admitted he mischaracterized the facts.

I handed him the second piece of evidence, and we repeated the exercise. Again, he refused to answer. This time I didn't have to say anything and simply looked at the judge, who instructed him to answer the question.

I handed him the third piece of evidence, and we repeated the exercise a third time. For the third time Mr. Duke refused to answer the question. The die was cast.

This time, I slowly folded my notebook, stepped back from where I had been standing, looked at the jury, and with a tone in my voice said, "Your honor, I don't have any other questions for this witness."

⅄ ⅄ ⅄

When plaintiff finished presenting his evidence and rested, the defense lawyers met to talk about what to do. Plaintiff had failed to prove much at all it turned out. They put in the letter, the incorrect interrogatory answer with "wrong" in the margin, and each of the parties testified about what they did or did not do. But they failed for some inexplicable reason to put the judgment Mr. Chaussee agreed to in evidence. They failed to put the insurance policy into evidence. It was as if they thought these were all admitted facts, which was not the case. Everybody talked about these things in opening statements, but the judge always tells the jury before and after opening statement that what the lawyers say is not evidence.

Without the judgment there was just no evidence to support a contention that Mr. Chaussee had been damaged, even under the rule that imagines the damage. We argued for dismissal on this ground and others. Our trial judge, Judge McCutcheon, said he agreed there was no evidence of damages, but he said, "I want to hear the defense case first."

We went into the jury room, which was empty at the end of the day, and conferred again. I argued to the rest of the defense lawyers that if we put on a defense by calling witnesses, the plaintiff's case would only improve. We had experts lined up to explain why the underlying case was a loser for plaintiff, and why there was no negligence or bad faith, despite the obvious errors. By putting on a case, plaintiff would be able to put on a rebuttal case. They had Jan Eric Petersen, the former president of the trial lawyer's association and zealous advocate for plaintiffs, disclosed as a rebuttal witness on all issues of liability and damages. Although I had considerable trial experience by then, I was still a mid-level associate. Bill Helsell had two experienced partners with him, and Maryland Casualty had three partners from two law firms. After thinking it over, they agreed with me to rest without presenting a defense case.

Judge McCutcheon was not happy, but he had been a seasoned trial lawyer before he went on the bench, and I'm sure he appreciated our ballsy move. He gave us a verdict form that had no place for the jury to state what the damages were. The verdict form asked, were the defendants negligent, and if so, did the negligence compel Mr. Chaussee to agree to enter the judgment? He was referring to the judgment that was not in evidence.

ᴧ　ᴧ　ᴧ

In final argument, I used an approach that I rely upon every time I'm in a trial and all the other parties have multiple lawyers in the court room. I prefer to try cases by myself. I'll ask for help in jury selection to take notes or to gauge the juror's responses, but when the trial gets under way, I like to be in control of what is said and by whom.

When it came time for my summation, I pointed to the other lawyers in the courtroom, and told the jury,

"You surely have noticed that all the parties other than my client have lots of lawyers here. Plaintiff has two lawyers, the insurance company has three lawyers, and the law firm has three lawyers. But I am here all by myself. Now, the advantage of having two lawyers on the case is that while one of them is up here talking, the other can be thinking. So please don't hold it against me if while I'm up here talking, nobody is thinking."

That story works every time. It does two things. It makes the jury laugh, and it gains a bit of sympathy for my plight. I really don't need any sympathy but it helps.

In my summation I spent most of my time dissecting Mr. Duke's report. It was the only evidence of the strength of the underlying case. I argued you could not believe anything in it because of the demonstrated fictions. I went at Mr. Duke as hard as I could.

Bill Helsell rose to give his summation when I was finished. He started out with an incredulous tone in his voice. He said, "In all my years in this business, I have never heard such things as Mr. Bond said about my client. I don't know where he got such ideas. I guess we'll just have to take his word for it that he was not thinking about what he was saying."

All eyes looked at me and I held up one finger to show: score one for Helsell.

The jury deliberated for five days, which is still the longest deliberation in a case I tried. The shortest was ten minutes. The jury answered both questions with "yes." Yes, our clients were negligent, and yes, that negligence compelled Mr. Chaussee to agree to the judgment. Well, that didn't work out quite the way I planned.

All parties proposed judgments on the jury verdict as if they won. Plaintiff proposed a judgment for $7.5 million, less the offset for the payments from King County and Maryland Casualty. Each of the defendants proposed judgments of dismissal. In our briefing and argument, we held the judge to his observation that there was no proof of damages.

The judge agreed with us and entered our orders of dismissal, and they were affirmed on appeal.

Chapter 4

Threatened with Arrest

"**H**ave you ever had sexual intercourse with Jack McDonald?" That was the first question I asked Carol Gabrielson at her deposition.

When taking a deposition, usually you start by asking the witness to state her name and address. I was hoping I might catch Mrs. Gabrielson off guard and she would be ashamed and answer "no", but she said "yes".

I followed up and asked, "How many times?"

With no shame whatsoever she said, "Fifty or sixty."

Her relationship with Pastor McDonald was the main issue in the case. Plaintiff's attorney, Dan Hannula, theorized that Mr. McDonald used his position as her pastor to seduce Mrs. Gabrielson into becoming his sexual slave. Her answers to the first questions at her deposition convinced me that they would be able to prove the sexual part of the case. As the suit evolved, exactly who seduced who became the issue.

⋏ ⋏ ⋏

The case arose at a time when the revelations about Reverend Jimmy Swaggart and Pastor Jim Baker were front page news. They were Southern evangelical preachers, full of hellfire and brimstone about sin and the need to repent or the gates to heaven would be closed forever. Both preachers built successful ministries. Then we learned their behavior was no better than the sinners they railed against, and they both crashed and burned in disgrace. Swaggart was said to have had a homosexual encounter with a young man. Swaggart condemned homosexual behavior as an abomination of God's word, and it was more than a little hypocritical for him to do what he damned others to hell for doing. And Baker, well, he just slept around with young women while his big-haired wife, Tammy Baker, raised millions of dollars for their church with teary-eyed televised pleas. The Bakers' dog house was said to be nicer than the homes of many the poor folks who sent them money. These publicized events and tabloid gossip provide the context for the case of *Gabrielson vs. McDonald.*

Pastor McDonald was the spiritual leader of the Community Chapel in Tacoma, a satellite church of a larger organization. A former well-driller from Montana, he came to preaching the Gospel late in life. Briefly, he dabbled in a theory that we can use our minds to control how plants grow. Sometime after he started preaching, the headquarters church began to preach about what they called "spiritual connections" and "deep love." Very often these deep spiritual connections became physical connections, and sometimes the two worshipers who connected as only a man and a woman can were married to someone else.

⅄ ⅄ ⅄

Carol Gabrielson was a simple and troubled woman. She showed goats at the state fair and married a hard working man named Ira. The calluses on Ira's hands were embedded with grease and dirt from his job as a mechanic at a U-Haul dealership. Her mother raised her in a Pentecostal church, but her father refused to go to church and he complained loudly when they came home after Sunday services. He accused his wife of having an affair with the church pastor and he called her vile names like "whore." Fearful of what might happen during these outbursts, Carol would flee to the woods behind their home and hide until the yelling stopped. And as if that wasn't enough to trouble a woman's soul, when her father was dying, Carol had to decide when to pull the plug to terminate his life support.

⋏ ⋏ ⋏

A Wikipedia entry says Donald Lee Barnett founded the Community Chapel while he was employed as a Boeing draftsman. He attended a Bible college in Idaho and then he started a Bible study, and one thing led to the next. After fifteen years or so, the Community Chapel had grown into a large church with a grade school, recording studio, satellite churches and a large and enthusiastic congregation. The services were evangelical and joyous. Some spoke in tongues during the services, and all who came to church there believed that these were the end times and only believers would enjoy the Rapture, when Jesus would arrive to gather up all who believed in Him.

It was also a big business with a bank account, a twenty-acre church property, vehicles, a school and employees, all governed by the church elders, including some senior business executives, who insured the church against liability with the CNA Insurance Company. In those days our law firm was the primary panel defense counsel for CNA.

⋏ ⋏ ⋏

Life, the nature of the services and preaching, and preparations for the end days began to boil at the Community Chapel. The services started to draw attention when a Catholic priest stood up one day and shouted that Satan was in their midst. After that disturbance the church employed plain-clothed security guards in suits to eject any more trouble makers. All the preaching about "spiritual connections" and the dancing that accompanied the services titillated the local print and television media who began to run stories about the Community Chapel.

The rate of divorce among the congregation soared, no doubt the result of all the extra-marital spiritual connections that were encouraged at services. Many men and women and their families were hurt, and some began to sue. I caught wind of this spurt of litigation and told the senior partner of our firm that if the claims come to our firm I'd like to handle them. A week later, Dave Martin came to my office with a stack of new files and said, "Here you go, Mike."

A half dozen women and their husbands sued the church and pastors claiming destruction of their marriages and emotional distress. In one case, a woman sued to get back a $5 million gift. As a teenager she had received a settlement for paraplegic injuries suffered in a car accident, and she gave it all to Barnett and the Community Chapel when it was just getting started. After she made the gift, her father sued them claiming undue influence. But the court dismissed the case at the end of the plaintiff's opening statement. She tried again many years later.

Washington, like many progressive states, had abolished the tort of alienation of affections, which permitted a jilted man or woman to sue the interloper who stole away his wife's or her husband's affections. In view of the state of the law, the plaintiffs had to dress up the claims under other theories.

The congregation at the Community Chapel was unorthodox for sure. Yet as wacky as the preaching and doctrine sounded, these folks had a constitutional right to believe what they wanted. In essence, it seemed to me that these cases amounted to an attack on a controversial religious order. The cases had an interesting constitutional rights dimension, loads of publicity, and Carol Gabrielson's case had a twist the others lacked. We tee'd up her case for trial.

ㅅ ㅅ ㅅ

The torrid love affair between Carol Gabrielson and Pastor McDonald began after she went to see him asking for help because she was unhappy in her marriage. Not too long afterwards, the counseling sessions began to include sexual intercourse, sometimes, they claimed, in the room next to where Gabrielson's husband and McDonald's wife were watching TV. Afterward they would agree what had transpired was wrong and sinful and should stop. They would pray for forgiveness, and promised each other they would never do that again, and then the next time they were together it would happen all over again. The temptations of the flesh were too strong.

After a couple months of lovemaking, Pastor McDonald, who was troubled more about it than Mrs. Gabrielson appeared to be, said that "enough was enough" and he refused to see her again. She wouldn't let him go so easily and embarrassed him at his Tacoma church on a few occasions. Unable to persuade her to keep quiet about the affair, Pastor McDonald put Mrs. Gabrielson out of the church, shunning her and excommunicating her from ever coming back to church again. That was a mistake. She became a woman scorned and all hell broke loose.

During the trial of the case, Brian Johnson of KOMO television news reported the story as a real-life "Fatal Attraction," referring to the 1987 movie, which portrays Michael Douglas as a man who comes to regret an affair he had. Like Glenn Close's character in the film, Mrs. Gabrielson went after the men who wronged her. After she was put out of the church, Mrs. Gabrielson went to the Community Chapel's home church, where she made a scene, yelling something like, "it's all lies. They will ruin you. Stay away from these evil people." The security guards forcibly removed her from the premises. But she didn't go easily and the security guards battered and bruised her in the confrontation.

She and her husband retained Tacoma attorney Dan Hannula, an All American swimmer at the University of Washington and successful plaintiff's counsel, and he filed suit in Pierce County Superior Court, alleging damages for counseling and pastoral negligence arising from her relationship with Pastor McDonald. She also claimed assault and battery for the injuries she suffered when the security guards dragged her kicking and screaming from the church services.

The insurance company appointed separate counsel for Pastor McDonald, and in the beginning I represented both Pastor Barnett and the Community Chapel Church. As the trial date approached, it became increasingly clear that a potential conflict of interest existed between Pastor Barnett and his church. A few months before the trial began I withdrew as counsel for the Pastor and remained in as counsel for the church.

ʎ ʎ ʎ

The claim that Pastor Barnett's preaching was causing marriages to break up seemed to me to be protected speech under the First Amendment. During Pastor Barnett's deposition, which happened to be early in the case, Mrs. Gabrielson's attorney, Mr. Hannula, began to ask about Barnett's personal love life, and I instructed the witness not to answer that question.

Instructing the witness not to answer a question in a deposition is a risky tactic and it usually causes quite a commotion. The lawyer who asked the question will not be happy with you and, sure enough, Mr. Hannula was visibly pissed off at my obstruction of his questioning. If nothing else is accomplished, this tactic will give you time to speak with the witness and remind him or her of the need to be truthful. The attorney needs to be aware of the risk that the witness will lie and create more trouble for him or herself. As President Nixon could attest, the cover-up is always worse than the crime. Nevertheless, instructing a client not to answer a deposition question should be employed only when grave dangers exist.

The greater risk of instructing a witness not to answer a deposition question is annoying the judge, who may be asked to rule on the issue, and that is what happened this time. Mr. Hannula's office was a short walk across the street from the courthouse, which was convenient when he wanted to go see the judge or check a court file, but it was very inconvenient for me in this circumstance. So we adjourned the deposition and marched across the street to argue about whether the witness should be ordered to answer the question.

The case had been assigned to Judge Gary Steiner, and he had a jury trial in session. I suspect Mr. Hannula's assistant called ahead to let them know we were coming, because as soon as we walked into the courtroom, Judge Steiner asked the witness to stand down and he told the jury to return to the jury room. After a short argument, the judge ordered the witness to answer the question. I don't recall exactly what the question was, but I had a feeling the answer was not going to help my client's cause.

In that situation, there were only two options: either answer all the questions truthfully or appeal.

When we returned to the conference room, I informed Mr. Hannula that we planned to appeal the judge's ruling. If he had other questions, he should ask them now; otherwise, we were finished for the afternoon.

He said, "I am not going to ask another question until I get answers to the questions that Judge Steiner ordered. If he does not answer the questions, then I am going right back over and obtain a contempt order."

Another impromptu hearing with this judge did not bode well, and I said, "Well, I am not going back to see the judge without a written motion and five days' notice." We left his office.

A fax was waiting for me when I returned to my office in Seattle. Mr. Hannula had gone over and persuaded Judge Steiner, *ex parte*, to sign an *order to show cause* why I should not be held in contempt of court, and if I did not appear on the date set, the order said the judge would issue a bench warrant for my arrest.

It hadn't occurred to me that I might get arrested for something like this. To be arrested for civil disobedience against the war or protesting government oppression would make going to jail a worthy sacrifice, but going to jail because I didn't want my client to answer a deposition question was not nearly so noble.

I appeared in Judge Steiner's court as he had ordered and humbly apologized. I made excuses about the high stakes, excessive publicity, and the right to privacy. He didn't impose any sanction, but he reiterated his ruling that the witness had to answer the questions; I think he understood that emotions were running hot in the case and maybe my zealous advocacy had interfered with my judgment. In the end, we did not appeal the ruling, the deposition never was resumed, and Pastor Barnett did not have to answer the questions that concerned me.

Later on I complained to the judge that discovery was out of control and proof was the fact that he had threatened me with arrest. He denied any knowledge of such a threat and when I showed him the *order to show cause*, he said he relies on the lawyers to give him properly written orders.

人 人 人

Three or four weeks before the trial was set to start, I received an anonymous tip that it would be useful to search the criminal records in Las Vegas. I retained a former FBI agent who was living in Las Vegas to look into the tip, and a week later he sent me a package of documents. It turned out that Pastor Barnett had been convicted of exposing himself to a housekeeper at the Circus Circus Hotel & Casino in Las Vegas. The package contained witness statements, the charges, and papers showing a guilty plea and small fine. This information presented a problem.

By now Pastor Barnett had separate counsel, Rodney Hollenback, and we worked together as best we could. Rodney was a gregarious, likable fellow who grew up in Colfax, Washington, a small farming town in southeast Washington. We had no reason to believe Mr. Hannula was aware of the Las Vegas episode, but it would have been reckless to proceed as if he did not know about it because the story would have a considerable impact if he was able to spring it on us in front of the jury during the trial. So we prepared a *motion in limine*.

Motions in limine are a technique by which the lawyers ask the judge to rule on evidentiary issues before trial begins. You can ask the judge to exclude the evidence completely; you can seek to exclude only part of the evidence; or you can prevent the evidence from being offered until something else comes into evidence. If the evidence is subject to a foundation or to other evidence that may not be offered, you might ask the judge to bar the other lawyer from saying anything about it in opening statement.

Sometimes you should seek an order in limine that limits what the other lawyer can say about the evidence. In a case in which an intoxicated driver was at least partially at fault for an accident, the driver's lawyer obtained an order in limine that prohibited anyone from referring to his client as a "drunk driver," as that was too inflammatory. He argued that the label was unfairly calculated to cause the jury to get angry at his client.

The rules of evidence say that relevant evidence is admissible, but the court can exclude relevant evidence if the probative value of the evidence is substantially outweighed by the danger of unfair prejudice or confusion of the issues. The evidence of Pastor Barnett's Las Vegas peccadillo was certainly capable of causing unfair prejudice and confusion. It probably was not relevant to any issue in the case, which concerned Pastor MacDonald's conduct and the injuries Carol Gabrielson suffered when she was dragged from the church kicking and screaming, not Pastor Barnett's conduct. To be on the safe side, we had to present the evidence to the trial judge and ask for a ruling barring its introduction into evidence.

ʎ ʎ ʎ

Not long after threatening me with arrest, Judge Steiner called us into his chambers to make a disclosure. Apparently, he didn't like the publicity the case was attracting; it seemed like we had television news cameras in the court room for every motion, and maybe he didn't like being on TV. He told us he looked at the witness lists and noticed that one of Mrs. Gabrielson's treating psychologists happened to be the daughter of his former law partner. He asked if any of us wanted him to recuse himself from the case. Each of the lawyers spoke and told him they saw no problem and would not ask for recusal. Then it was my turn to speak.

I said, "Judge, what concerns me is that it concerns you; so I think it might be best if you *did* recuse yourself."

He asked, "Is there anything else that is bothering you?" He might have been thinking I was still peeved about the threat to arrest me.

I said, "Yes, there is judge, but I would just as soon keep it to myself because I will have to appear before you again someday."

He recused himself and the case was re-assigned to Tom Swayze, who granted our motion in limine.

⅄ ⅄ ⅄

Sometimes the trial lawyer's best work happens in the judge's chambers when you are technically off the record. Very often toward the end of a trial the judge will ask the lawyers to meet in chambers after regular hours to review the jury instructions, which inform the jury about the principles of the law they are to apply in deciding to the case. The best trial judges will take the lawyer's submissions of jury instructions and assemble a package of what he or she thinks the instructions should say. Then, a day or so before the evidence concludes, the judge will give the lawyers an informal chance to persuade him or her to take something out or put something in or say it differently. After this informal discussion is finished, the judge will assemble a set of jury instructions. Then the lawyers for both sides will go on the record with the court reporter and "take exceptions." Exceptions are the legal objections with citations to cases to the giving or failing to give a particular instruction for purposes of a later appeal.

In the *Corcoran* case, a product liability case, we had a complex set of legal issues about whether the Product Liability Act applied to two contractors who built an office building. An electrical panel in the building exploded many years later and burned the plaintiff. This plaintiff had two lawyers, and there were three defendants, each with their own lawyer. When we approached the end of the case, Judge Steve Scott gave us his package of instructions and invited us into chambers to talk about them.

The plaintiff's attorney, Tom Chambers, went first with his suggestions, and then each of us had the opportunity to comment on Tom's suggestions. Tom's brilliant associate, Andy Hoyle, went second, and then each of us was allowed to comment on his suggestions. And so it went for defense attorneys Linda Foreman and Doug Hoffman; they made their arguments and each of us in turn commented on the proposal. I was last. Everything that needed to be said had been said by that point.

When my turn came I said, "Judge, I've been looking over these jury instructions for the last hour or so, and I have to tell you I wouldn't change a thing. They are the best instructions I've ever seen!" Everybody had a good laugh.

入 入 入

In Mrs. Gabrielson's case, her lawyers planned to call a well-respected forensic psychiatrist, Dr. Phil Lindsay, to testify about liability and the psychic damage inflicted on her by Pastor MacDonald's behavior. Dr. Lindsay told us in deposition about the phenomenon known as *repetition compulsion*. According to the theory of repetition compulsion, as adults we tend to repeat very unpleasant events that happened to us in our childhood. He told us all about the verbal abuse inflicted by Mrs. Gabrielson's father when she came home from church. Dr. Lindsay said he found no evidence of sexual abuse, but he was confident that if he put Carol under deep enough hypnosis, he would uncover evidence of that, too.

I retained Dr. Richard Carter, psychiatrist, to assist me in the evaluation of Mrs. Gabrielson's claims and Dr. Lindsay's testimony. Dr. Carter's review gave the case an entirely new complexion.

Plaintiff's theory of the case was that Pastor MacDonald had seduced Mrs. Gabrielson into becoming his sexual slave. In large part, they used Dr. Lindsay to present that claim because he had extensive experience with sexual abuse of minors. Dr. Lindsey explained the techniques of grooming that abusers use with their victims. A vulnerable person seeks help from a respected person in a position of authority, who then gradually insinuates himself into the most intimate parts of her life, gains her trust, and then he asks her to do things that are shameful. *Gabrielson vs. MacDonald* was, in his opinion, a classic case of grooming followed by sexual abuse all within the guise of the pastor's marriage counseling.

Dr. Carter saw things differently. Picking up on the theory of repetition compulsion, he told me that in his view, not only had Mrs. Gabrielson not been seduced by Pastor MacDonald but she, in fact, seduced him. He concluded she did so in order to test the truth of the allegation that her father made against her mother. When Mrs. Gabrielson and her mother came home from church, her father would accuse her mother of having an affair with their pastor. Mrs. Gabrielson needed to know if it was true, and she set about to find out by trying to seduce Pastor MacDonald.

It was great fun to present this testimony in the defense case. Dr. Carter's direct and cross-examination took a full day of trial. The jury watched the testimony intently as if it was an Oscar-winning movie.

⅄ ⅄ ⅄

The new trial judge, Judge Swayze, excluded the evidence from Las Vegas, proving the truth of the ad campaign: "What happens in Vegas, stays in Vegas."

Judge Swayze also helped us during trial at one key moment. I needed someone to present the church doctrine in a manner that made it sound more mainstream and less controversial than the newspapers and television reports and Mr. Hannula were trying to portray it. The Pastor of the Yakima satellite church, Father O'Brien, was the perfect witness. He was a former Catholic priest, spoke with a hint of Irish in his voice, and he was the picture of virtue. He had a way of speaking about "spiritual connections" that made the concept sound wholesome and Biblical. In preparing for his testimony I made it clear to him that we were going to tell the jury only about the doctrine and that he should be very careful to say nothing about the services. In contrast to my usual practice, I mapped out a carefully structured direct examination.

As I walked Father O'Brien through his direct testimony, I carefully limited all my questions to the doctrine, to what Pastor Barnett had said, and I avoided any question that would insert the actual practices – at church or otherwise – into the case.

On cross-examination, after trying to poke holes in the testimony about the doctrine and preaching, Mr. Hannula asked with a sneering tone of disgust, "Well, did he practice what he preached?"

I immediately objected to the question as it was beyond the scope of the direct examination. As a general rule of trial practice, the cross-examination of a witness is supposed to be limited to the scope of the direct examination, but some trial judges enforce this rule more rigorously than others. The danger is "opening the door" to cross examination by treading too closely to the line of questioning you want to avoid. Although I had asked about doctrine, not the practice, Judge Swayze overruled my objection. Before Father O'Brien could answer the question, I asked for a hearing out of the presence of the jury. Judge Swayze sent the jury into the jury room, and we argued about the issue.

I said, "Your honor, I structured my direct examination of Father O'Brien very carefully to limit the scope of his testimony to the doctrine, and at no time did I ask him to testify about the services or the actual practices of Pastor Barnett or anyone else."

Judge Swayze asked the court reporter to read back portions of my direct examination and then he said, "Mr. Bond your objection is well taken. I was mistaken and your objection is sustained."

I don't recall trying a case with a trial judge before or since then who was as careful as Judge Swayze.

人 人 人

Cross-examination is an art that takes practice. Irving Younger, a noted trial practice instructor, uses ten rules of cross-examination. While every trial lawyer should study those rules, the best way to learn how to cross-examine is to find opportunities to conduct a cross-examination.

The first rule of cross-examination in those days was, "don't." Too often, a cross-examination causes more damage than good. In fact, if you don't have the ammunition to decimate the witness or draw out some helpful testimony, your case will be better off if you just leave it alone and avoid drawing attention to the testimony. In all events, you do not want to give the witness a chance to simply repeat the damaging testimony. One of Professor Younger's rules is to listen to what the witness says. As it happened, I had a good opportunity to put that rule to use in another asbestos case.

In those days, our client was on the verge of bankruptcy due to the thousands of cases it was defending all around the country. The costs of defense were astronomical, and in order to reduce its defense costs, the client prohibited the defense lawyers from taking any more depositions of the plaintiff's expert witnesses. Many of these witnesses had been deposed hundreds of times, and usually it was not difficult to predict what they might say. In one case, the partner in charge of the litigation handed me the file hours before the trial began and I saw we had no depositions of expert witnesses.

One of plaintiff's experts, an industrial hygienist, was very damaging to us in his direct examination; we had no prior depositions or reports, and I was uneasy about exactly what I was going to do with this guy. When the plaintiff's attorney finished his direct examination, the trial judge, Judge Robert Lasnik, said I could cross-examine the witness.

I said, "Your honor, I will reserve my cross-examination until the defense case." I was thinking that back at the office I could plan how I was going to dismantle the witness's direct testimony.

Judge Lasnik replied, "What was that again?"

I repeated, "Your honor, I would like to reserve my cross-examination to the defense case."

Judge Lasnik said, "Can we have a sidebar?" A sidebar is a conference with the judge out of the hearing of the jury so the lawyer can try to persuade the judge to change his mind about a ruling he just made. In hindsight, asking me for a sidebar was a generous approach because usually it is the lawyers who ask the judge for one. But we were trying all kinds of new things that day.

Judge Lasnik asked me to repeat exactly what I had in mind again, and after I told him what I wanted to do for what was the third time, he asked, "Is this witness on your witness list?"

"No, your honor, he is not," I replied.

Judge Lasnik said, "Well if you want to cross-examine the witness then you will have to do so right now because I am not bringing him back."

As a result, I was forced to think on my feet, and listen very carefully to what the witness said.

$$\lambda \quad \lambda \quad \lambda$$

As the trial of *Gabrielson vs. McDonald* progressed, a witness appeared who moved me to stunned silence. Pastor MacDonald's attorney told me she found a witness that she thought would be very helpful. In those days, we were not subject to case schedules and discovery cutoffs and all the other pretrial procedures that serve mostly to limit what surprises can happen at trial.

A gentleman named Ed McHugh took the stand. He was dressed in black trousers and a black shirt open at the collar. He had a pencil thin, dark beard and mustache. When seated on the witness stand, he took a comfortable pose, sitting back with his arms resting on the railings on either side as if he was in an easy chair. He sat with his legs spread wide apart. He told the jury a story of sweet love gone sour.

He met Carol Gabrielson through a dating service, and they arranged to meet at a diner for coffee one evening. After coffee they went to his house and sat on his sofa and began to kiss. They kissed and they kissed and then, he said, they went to his bedroom and began to make love.

His story was beginning to sound pretty good. The jury was watching intently. I was wondering where she was going with this witness.

He said, "We made love, and then we made love some more and we made love until I couldn't make love anymore."

McDonald's lawyer asked, "Did you say anything at that point?

He said, "Yes, I told Carol I had to get something to eat because I had to go to work."

"What did she say?"

With a proud tone of voice and stretching his legs just a little farther apart, he said, "She seemed to be particularly interested in the size of my penis."

As Dana Carvey's Church Lady might have said, "Weeellllllll, isn't that special?"

I was taking notes and looked up at the witness, the jury, and the judge who kept a pretty good poker face on. I wasn't doing so well. I could not believe what I just heard. Right, she called this witness to tell the jury about his, his big dick? What on earth is she thinking? I wasn't sure how this was helping our case. Should I do something? Should I jump up and ask for an offer of proof?

McDonald's lawyer told me on the break that she was just as surprised as I was. She thought he was going to tell us about how Mrs. Gabrielson began to threaten the man. Later it came out that when he refused to see her any more, she threw a rock through his window with a threatening note attached. All that and the threatening note eventually came into evidence, which on one level supported the defense theory that she was just a scorned woman.

When the judge asked me if I had any questions, I was unable to look up from my notes and I applied Professor Younger's first rule of cross-examination and just shook my head "no." Ever since that day, I've wished I had the presence of mind to say, "Your honor, I'm not going to touch that one with a ten-foot pole!"

ʎ ʎ ʎ

The case and trial had been a roller coaster from the beginning. At one point while Mr. Hannula was examining Pastor MacDonald about his background, he offered into evidence a pamphlet claiming to teach techniques of mind control over plants. The media were having a field day with the trial about a pastor who tricked a woman into being his sexual slave. Television cameras were in the courtroom throughout the trial, and stories appeared in the local papers every day.

At the conclusion of the evidence, Judge Swayze dismissed the claims against Pastor Barnett because he didn't do anything other than preach. Plaintiff's claims against Pastor Macdonald and the church as his employer were submitted to the jury.

In argument, I complained about what I called an un-American attack on a controversial church and the need for freedom of worship and religion. I argued about the Salem witch trials, how Mr. Hannula was out to get this church because he didn't like it, and how Mrs. Gabrielson wasn't tricked into becoming a sexual slave, but instead she was a willing participant until the adults around her finally said, "This is wrong." When the verdict came in, I hurried back to Tacoma to be present when it was announced.

When I walked into the court room I saw Mr. Hannula and asked to speak with him in the stairwell in private. I put out my hand and said, "Dan, whatever happens, I hope you know I meant nothing personal."

He's a big guy and shook my hand firmly and said, "Thanks Mike, I know that. You're a hell of a lawyer and I don't want to go through anything like this again."

As I recall, the jury awarded $180,000 in damages to Mrs. Gabrielson and her husband for the abuse of the counseling relationship with Pastor MacDonald, and they reduced the award by one-third for the contributory negligence on her part. Dr. Carter's testimony proved useful in the end. On the other claim for assault and battery for ejecting Mrs. Gabrielson from the services that night after she was put out of the Pastor MacDonald's Tacoma church, the jury found in favor of the Community Chapel. The security guards used no more force than was reasonably necessary.

Two days later, Marianne and I were sitting on a beach in Maui drinking cold beverages with little umbrellas, and I was thinking that was quite a ride.

Chapter 5

Three Cases of Defamation

The law of defamation provides a private cause of action for damages that may be recovered by the victim of the defamatory statement. Slander occurs in oral statements; libel occurs in writing. Defamation requires damage to reputation and it is one of the few torts that do not require proof of out of pocket damages.

Unless you represent newspapers or other media clients, most lawyers will never encounter a claim of defamation. I've been lucky to try three defamation cases to verdict, and there were legal and life lessons in all three. The alleged victims were a locksmith, a neighbor in a small community, and a political campaign worker.

There are four elements to prove a case of defamation:

1. a false statement,
2. fault, which means the speaker or writer knew or should have known the statement was false,
3. an unprivileged context, and
4. damage to reputation.

⋏ ⋏ ⋏

In my first defamation case, when a lady I'll call Regina came home one day she believed she had locked her keys in her car. She called a locksmith to come and open her car. A Korean fellow responded to the call, and she waited in the house while he worked. After he opened the car, he said he found no keys in the ignition. Regina did not understand how that could be true. But she needed a car key and she asked the locksmith make her a new key. After he left, she called the police and reported that the locksmith had stolen her keys. She was sure he had hidden the keys after he opened the car and he must have used it as a ruse to get an extra $100 out of her.

The police went to talk to the locksmith about the alleged theft. He denied her claim. He refused to refund the $100, and the cops referred the case to the prosecutor. The prosecutor, who may not have had enough to do that week, charged the locksmith with theft. The defendant took the case to trial, and the jury found him not guilty. The locksmith then sued Regina for defamation.

I had defended Regina's uncle, a lawyer named CC, in a legal malpractice claim a few years earlier, and he referred his niece to me. Many clients have come to ask for my help this way. If you do a good job for one client and treat them like you care about their problem and get lucky, then they know who to send their friends and family to with a legal problem.

In her uncle's case, CC put a down-on-her-luck divorced lady through a bankruptcy for a flat fee of $450. Although she had no income and was a very poor manager of what limited funds she did have, she owned a house free and clear, and it had substantial equity. The utility companies had cut off her power and water for non-payment of the utility bills long before she hired CC. She ran an extension cord from the neighbor's house so she could watch TV and run the refrigerator.

CC's client sold the house in the bankruptcy, received $200,000 in cash, and promptly gave it away to her two good for nothing adult sons. After she lost everything, she hired a lawyer who claimed CC was negligent for filing the bankruptcy, even though that is what she instructed him to do. The new lawyer said all she needed was credit counseling. At trial they asked for damages of $225,000. I was somewhat panicked when her lawyer asked the jury for $225,000 because they didn't claim more than $125,000 before trial began, and that is what I told CC's insurer was the worst case outcome. The jury's verdict came in with an award of $225.00.

The bailiff read the verdict, "We, the jury, find for the plaintiff for two hundred and twenty-five .... dollars," and she made a long dramatic pause between "five" and "dollars." I thought my ears were playing tricks on me, but that is what they said: $225.

In speaking with the jury afterward, I asked them how they came to arrive at damages of $225. The jury chairwoman said, "We concluded the plaintiff did not get all the legal advice she paid for, so we refunded one-half the fee." As amusing as it is, this is one reason why I gave up talking to jurors after the verdict comes in. It is just too scary.

Regina, who needed a lawyer to defend the Korean locksmith's suit for defamation, called me on CC's recommendation.

Like many states, Washington adopted a statute called Anti-SLAPP which is an acronym for Strategic Lawsuits Against Public Participation; an Anti-SLAPP statute grants immunity to citizens who give information to the government in certain cases. Although the immunity from suit is usually intended to encourage citizens to dispute governmental actions like zoning or land-use decisions without fear of becoming embroiled in a defamation lawsuit, the immunity also applies in many other contexts, such as when people make complaints to the police. Under the Anti-SLAPP statute, in addition to the usual elements of a claim for defamation, the victim must prove the false statement was made with malice.

Proving malice is tough for the plaintiff because the burden of proof of malice is by "clear and convincing evidence," which is something more than "a preponderance of the evidence." Preponderance is the standard of proof in an ordinary civil case. These hurdles, including proof of a false statement ("I did not steal her keys"), the speaker's knowledge of the falsity ("She knew I did not steal her keys"), proof of malice, and damage to reputation, and possibly limited damages, make these cases unattractive to your usually hungry plaintiff's attorney.

Under our civil rules, the case was subject to a mandatory arbitration, first. The Korean locksmith and his lawyer appeared at the arbitration with an interpreter. His lawyer claimed the locksmith needed an interpreter to communicate effectively. I believe the tactic of using an interpreter was intended to interfere in any cross-examination because he seemed to understand and speak English just fine when I took his deposition. The appointed arbitrator was a gruff old defense lawyer who wasn't going to put up with any of this interpreter bullshit. He ordered the interpreter to leave and, after hearing the evidence, promptly ruled in Regina's favor.

Plaintiff sought a trial *de novo* in the superior court. By the time we got to final argument, the issue was whether Regina made the police report with malice. The jury answered that question "no," but they were deeply conflicted about what they thought was an injustice done to the Korean. Before they left the jury box, several of the jurors apologized to him in open court after the bailiff announced the verdict.

λ   λ   λ

In the *Hoechlin* case, my client was a handwriting expert, or to be more precise, a documents examiner. I was retained to handle an appeal of the trial court ruling that the anti-SLAPP statute did not apply to the case. After the appeal succeeded we tried the case on the issue of malice. The suit should never have been filed in the first place.

The claims arose from a squabble among retirees who lived in a small community on the Washington coast. The fight was over the origin of unwanted magazines, other mail, and free mail order gifts. One of the couples in the neighborhood were thorns in the side of one or two of their neighbors, all of whom were members of the same community club. Inundated with the unwanted magazines and mail order gifts, the thorny couple believed someone was forging their names on the mail order cards. They wanted to know who was doing it, and they retained my client because she was an experienced documents examiner and forensic handwriting expert. I'll call her Kathy Dean.

Kathy Dean was retained to evaluate the handwriting on the mail order cards with known examples of the handwriting of several neighbors, including a woman named Bobbi Hoechlin. Ms. Dean concluded that it was "highly probable" that Mrs. Hoechlin was the forger, though she could not say her opinion was beyond a reasonable doubt. The thorny victims of this great forgery communicated Ms. Dean's opinions to the county prosecuting attorney, and he promptly filed forgery charges against Mrs. Hoechlin. It seemed once again that the local authorities didn't have enough to do that week.

Mrs. Hoechlin's attorney contacted Ms. Dean, who agreed to sign an affidavit in which she said she could not say beyond a reasonable doubt that Mrs. Hoechlin was the forger. A criminal case called *Knapsted* says if the prosecution relies on expert testimony, the expert must be certain of her opinions beyond a reasonable doubt, or the case should be dismissed. And based on Ms. Dean's affidavit, the forgery charges against Bobbi Hoechlin were dismissed.

Lest no good deed go unpunished, Mrs. Hoechlin and her erstwhile lawyer filed a civil suit for defamation against Ms. Dean. Mrs. Hoechlin made several other claims against the prosecutor, the police, and several neighbors, but by the time the case came to me, all other claims had been settled or dismissed. The case against Ms. Dean had been dismissed on the grounds that in Washington expert witnesses are absolutely immune from liability arising from their work or opinions in a court case. That rule is an off-shoot from the immunity granted to judges. Her counsel at that time also argued for immunity under the anti-SLAPP statute. Although the statute provides a right to attorney fees if you prevail, the judge ruled that the statute did not apply. I was retained to appeal that issue, and the ruling barring recovery of attorney fees under the statute was reversed. The case was remanded for a trial on the issue of whether my client had acted with malice.

The case was pending in Grays Harbor County Superior Court in Montesano, Washington.

Built during the Great Depression in the 1930's, the courtroom ceilings in that building are high, as they are in all the old courthouses built during that era. The entrance hallways lie below a magnificent rotunda that features large heroic paintings of local farm and logging scenes. The courtrooms have a separate "Attorneys Only" door. Huge paintings of ancient Greek or Roman domestic images hang on either side of the judge's bench. The majesty of the courthouse makes it a special place to try a case, much more so than the small, sterile and windowless courtrooms built in the 1950's and '60s. An interior photo of one of the courtrooms is on the cover of this book.

We tried the case to the bench, without a jury. By this time, the lawyer who filed the defamation suit had crashed and burned with mental health and substance abuse issues. He was suspended from practice, and a new lawyer took over and tried the case. The judge ruled for Ms. Dean the minute the evidence was concluded. Later we received a substantial award of attorney fees and costs.

I had learned somehow that Mrs. Hoechlin's husband was a retired Marine, and you don't have to be around me too long before you'll learn I was a Marine, too. As the saying goes, "Once a Marine, always a Marine." He caught me at the courthouse entrance after the judge ruled and he said they felt badly it had come this far. He thought his lawyer had not done the right things, and it seemed to me without doubt he was correct in his assessment. Too many times, I've met folks who were seriously abused by the incompetent lawyers they entrusted. He said they knew a large bill for my attorney fees was coming and it concerned them. They had nothing other than their home, his small pension, and social security. I said, "Make the best offer you can without ruining you and your wife. Tell me that is the best you can do, and I'll advise the client to accept it." He did what I asked, and the case settled.

It is important to remember that each case involves people whose lives have been disrupted in some way. Very few people want to take their problems to court, not only because doing so is expensive, but also because the courtroom is a public and somewhat alien setting. Most of the people you see in the courthouse are poor or of modest means. Usually half the crowd is there for a criminal matter, a DUI, a domestic violence complaint, or a drug offense, and these folks are rarely, if ever, among the affluent. The poor go to court to seek justice. Sometimes a large corporation or business finds itself in court, but often those disputes are arbitrated or mediated outside of court in a comfortable conference room. I'm not going to debate here the question as to whether that kind of private justice is a public good, but all aspiring trial lawyers should think about it. Our clients are real people and going to court is the last thing they want to do.

ʎ ʎ ʎ

Some very personal human stories arose in my third defamation trial.

The need to prove malice can arise in a defamation case another way. Sometimes the right to be free from false statements made about you is at odds with a person's First Amendment rights under the Constitution to say anything he or she wants to say. While we've all heard of Justice Oliver Wendell Holmes's admonition that there is no constitutional right to cry "Fire!" in a public theater that is not on fire, what about calling a politician a wife beater?

In 1964 in *New York Times v. Sullivan*, the U.S. Supreme Court ruled that somebody who is a "public figure" must prove malice in establishing a case for defamation. Apparently, the reason for this policy is that "robust speech" is necessary when the subject of discussion is a politician or other person in the public eye. Allowing robust free speech in a democracy ensures a full and fair airing of political differences. In other words, the argument goes, democracy suffers when it is too easy for a public figure to mount a claim for defamation. Consequently, when a false statement is made about a public figure, the victim of the false statement must prove not only that the statement was false, he or she must also prove the statement was made knowingly with malice.

ʎ ʎ ʎ

The case of *Brecht vs. Hague* concerned all these issues and more. Paul Brecht tried to help his friend, Richard Pope, in his campaign for the King County Council seat that was occupied by longtime Councilwoman, Jane Hague. Mr. Pope was a colorful figure, a lawyer and an unsuccessful candidate for public office several times. The Pope campaign launched a relentless attack against Ms. Hague for various transgressions including campaign contribution reporting violations (for which she paid a fine), misstatements about her education, and they insinuated that there were other reasons to question Ms. Hague's integrity and competence. For the most part Mr. Pope didn't attack Ms. Hague's votes or policy positions; he attacked her personally.

The campaign duel took place on Internet blogs, a local talk radio show, television reports, and in mailers sent to the voters' mailboxes at home.

Mr. Pope handled Mr. Brecht's divorce many years in the past, and the divorce file became useful to the Hague campaign when Mr. Brecht surfaced as a vocal supporter of Mr. Pope's election. He may have been Mr. Pope's only vocal supporter. The skeleton in Mr. Brecht's closet gave the Hague campaign a way to fight back.

The divorce court file contained seven affidavits signed by Mr. Brecht's former wife in which she stated that he was abusive to her throughout the marriage. According to the affidavits, he committed numerous acts of domestic violence, caused her bodily harm, and put her in fear of bodily injury many times. He was described as having a terrible temper. She said, "He hit me in front of our children. I called the police several times, but didn't press charges until the end of the marriage."

Drawing upon this information, Hague's campaign consultants prepared a mailer and sent it to roughly twenty thousand voters in the district. The mailer stated that "Paul

Brecht tops Pope's endorsement list. Brecht also tops law enforcement's list with multiple domestic violence arrests and at least one assault conviction." The problem was that the local police department kept no "law enforcement list," and Mr. Brecht was not convicted of assault. He had been arrested exactly twice and had pled guilty to violating a No Contact Order, not to an assault. That charge was dismissed in a plea bargain.

A few days after the mailer was delivered to the Sixth District voters, Mr. Pope filed the defamation lawsuit, ostensibly on behalf of Mr. Brecht against Ms. Hague and the campaign consultants. *The Seattle Post-Intelligencer* and *King 5 News* reported on the lawsuit the next day; *The Seattle Times* and *King 5 News* reported on the lawsuit the day after that. In the election the following week, Ms. Hague was re-elected. The lawsuit languished. Eventually Mr. Pope was suspended from the practice of law, and two years later, new counsel appeared for Mr. Brecht. Shortly thereafter I was retained to represent the campaign consultants.

In pretrial rulings, a judge determined that Mr. Brecht's vocal advocacy on blogs and his public endorsement of Mr. Pope made him a "qualified public figure" within the meaning of the Supreme Court's decision in *Sullivan vs. New York Times*. Consequently, the defamation claim fell within the rule that required proof of malice.

At trial we planned to argue for the defense that the gist or sting of the mailer was true and that any mistake was made without malice. As Mr. Brecht had no reputation – good or bad – among the district's voters, it also seemed clear to me that any harm to reputation was caused not by the defendants, but instead by Mr. Pope's tactic of ensuring the defamatory statements were broadcast by the newspaper and television news reports to all of

Western Washington. To show that the gist or sting of the incorrect statements were true, we planned to introduce every one of the affidavits Mr. Brecht's former wife had filed in the divorce case.

A few weeks before the trial began, Mr. Brecht's lawyer informed us he planned to perpetuate the former wife's testimony in a video deposition for use at trial. This seemed like a helpful idea. It is often difficult to get witnesses to appear for testimony on the day you want. If the testimony is on video tape and "in the can," then you can present it when it fits the rest of the case presentation, and there will be no surprises about what the witness is going to say. In this case, the surprise came during the deposition.

Mr. Brecht's lawyer began questioning the former Mrs. Brecht by introducing her and then asking her about her background, her former relationship with Mr. Brecht, and the emotional impact the mailer's statements had on him. After finishing these preliminaries, Mr. Brecht's lawyer began to question her about the many affidavits she had filed in the divorce case. She identified her signature, acknowledged the content of each affidavit and then said, "They were untrue. They were false claims."

Our cross-examination nailed that coffin shut. "You swore under penalties of perjury that Mr. Brecht had beaten you; isn't that right?"

She replied, "Yes."

I asked, "That he was physically violent toward you?"

"Yes."

"You filed this affidavit because you wanted the Court to believe that didn't you?"

"Yes."

"You wanted the Court to rely on that?"

"Yes."

"You wanted the Court to give you sole custody of the children; isn't that right?"

"Yes."

"So your testimony today that you've just talked about, the seven declarations, you lied in seven declarations that you filed with the court?"

"Yes."

During the trial, Judge John Ehrlich was upset to hear her testimony. Custody fights in the course of a divorce are the most difficult cases to decide, he told us. The husband and wife say diametrically opposite things, which cannot be true at the same time. To have the wife come in later and give sworn testimony that the sworn testimony she submitted in the divorce case was lies – well, he found it disturbing, to say the least. We were content with the problem in any event because nobody looked good: not Mr. Brecht, not the witness, not Mr. Pope and not the lawyer who asked her to say these things.

What about Mr. Brecht's lawyer? When he put her up to this, did he owe the former wife a duty to inform her that perjury was a crime? Should he have recommended that she seek counsel because she was about to either admit or commit perjury? In my view, lawyers should take more care to avoid asking witnesses to commit crimes, even if it helps the client.

It was not at all clear that this testimony would, in fact, help Mr. Brecht. He was trying to prove he was not a "wife beater," but the mailer didn't say he was a wife beater. It said "Brecht . . . tops law enforcement's list with multiple domestic violence arrests and at least one assault conviction." And it was going to be an admitted fact that the mailer was mistaken.

⅄ ⅄ ⅄

Another odd thing occurred during jury selection. For cases that involve high publicity or sensitive issues, it can be useful to ask the judge to require the prospective jurors to answer a written questionnaire asking if they have any information that could have an impact on the case. The trial lawyer needs to know if the juror's life experiences may be in play when they decide the case. If you can't work the juror's statements into a legitimate challenge for cause with your follow up questions, then a peremptory challenge may be necessary.

The trial of *Brecht vs. Hague* was going to involve allegations of domestic violence. It was hard to predict what impact a personal experience with abuse might have on this case. Too many women have been subjected to abuse by a man in their lives to think it wasn't going to have any impact on the case. So we used a questionnaire that asked, in part, if the allegations of domestic violence or abuse were an issue that they personally knew something about. If so, they were to say whether it was something they would prefer to talk about outside the presence of the other jurors. Three women answered "yes" to both questions.

The judge brought them into the court room for individual *voir dire* outside the presence of the others. Each of them said they were either the victim of abuse of some form or had witnessed it. They said they would prefer not to think about it or deal with it again and asked to be excused from serving. Without asking us, which would not have been necessary in any event, Judge Ehrlich said, "Yes, of course, I am sorry to have asked you to relive any part of it."

Jury selection took a full day and a half. When we came back to resume *voir dire* the next morning, I began my questions by addressing the group of prospective jurors about the questions the first day. I said, "After you got home last night, did anybody think of something about any of the things that came up yesterday? Is there anything that you thought we might want to know about?" I always start out the second day of jury selection with this question and it usually draws a response.

One gentleman in the back row raised his hand and said, "Yes, the questionnaire asked about any personal experiences with domestic violence or abuse. I remembered last night that many years ago a friend of mine was accused of abusing his daughter, and he committed suicide." That was dramatic enough, but then the fellow sitting next to him said, "You know what, the same thing happened to me. A neighbor friend was accused of some kind of abuse in the family, and he killed himself." Fortunately, it ended there. If one more guy raised his hand I would have thought I'd entered the Twilight Zone.

人　人　人

A very unusual trial tactic occurred during *voir dire*. Mr. Brecht's lawyer began his questions by saying to the general pool of prospective jurors, "Now, once I was disciplined by the Washington State Bar Association for an ethical violation. Will you hold that against my client?" There was no chance that any of these jurors knew about it until he told them. I knew him and was unaware of it.

I looked up at Judge Ehrlich. His eyes were looking my way intently. I am pretty sure he was looking for an objection. The purpose of *voir dire* is to learn things about the juror, not to teach the jury things about the lawyers. The judge would have sustained an objection on the grounds that the question does nothing to determine the juror's qualifications. It was such an odd thing to say that I let it go without objection. The judge looked at me intently for an objection again later in the trial.

The evidence came in about as expected. Before trial we filed a large number of motions in limine to exclude or limit the evidence and arguments that might be made. These included motions to prevent arguments asking the jury to "clean up" politics, arguments about the relative financial situation of the parties, asking the jury to be the conscience of the community or to make moral judgments, and barring expressions of personal belief by counsel. In final argument, Mr. Brecht's attorney violated nearly every pretrial order in limine. He went so far overboard in his argument that the judge instructed us to brief a demand for sanctions after the verdict was delivered.

Ms. Hague's attorney and I jumped up to object at first. The judge was visibly upset that his orders were so blatantly ignored. He sustained our objections and ordered the jury to disregard the statements. Toward the end of his argument, Mr. Brecht's attorney continued to make these outrageous assertions that were clearly intended to invite the jury to get mad at the defendants. The last few times when I looked up and saw the judge imploring me with his eyes to object, I shook my head to signal "no." Sometimes an advocate can go too far, and this one had crossed the line long ago. The more he said, the less credible he became. It was better to give him all the rope he needed to hang himself.

The jury found that the statements in the mailer were defamatory, but they also found no malice. The end result was that Judge Ehrlich entered a judgment in favor of the defendants. Eventually the case settled, and even that came about oddly.

The extent of damages was an issue throughout the case. The cases say the victim of defamation is entitled to an award of damages even where there is no proof of out-of-pocket costs, like lost wages or medical expenses. The damages in a case like this essentially were general damages, and it is easy to see that the more egregious the defamation or the more malicious the malice, the greater the general damages award might be. Before trial Mr. Brecht demanded hundreds of thousands of dollars to settle. While the jury was deliberating, we offered $80,000 in settlement, but he rejected the offer. After the verdict came in, we offered $5,000 in settlement. This offer was also rejected. Mr. Brecht filed a notice of appeal, and we offered $2,500 in settlement, and this offer was rejected. A few weeks later, Mr. Brecht called me and said he would settle for $500. We accepted his offer.

Several months later, Mr. Brecht filed a second suit against my client's first lawyer, alleging he had conspired in the defamation at issue in *Brecht vs. Hague*. I was retained again, the case was dismissed on summary judgment, and the court of appeals affirmed the dismissal without oral argument.

Chapter 6

Leaking Windows

When I first met Richard Fowler, he told me a story and I knew then that if the story came into evidence and we had an all woman jury, it was very likely we would win no matter what else happened.

He and his wife, Louvette, had been sued for alleged fraud, breach of contract, and negligence arising from their sale of a large waterfront home on the shore of Lake Washington in Medina. The Fowlers were insured by one of our firm's clients. I got the case and Fowler came in to my office to see if I was an acceptable choice for his counsel. Although the insurance company reserves the right to assign counsel of its choosing, the Rules of Professional Conduct prohibit a lawyer from taking on a client who does not consent to the representation. I think it is good practice always to obtain the client's written consent to representation.

We sat down together and chatted a bit. He began by describing the property, which he said was "a very large and complex property, not unlike a small hotel. You really must treat it as if it was a small hotel." We talked for a while. Born in Scotland and raised in Australia, he looked and sounded like the actor Sean Connery. I liked him immediately and I told him about my experience with construction cases. He liked my approach and consented to have me as his lawyer. He's been a good friend and client ever since our first meeting.

⅄ ⅄ ⅄

The claims involved a 16,000 square foot home on three levels, with an indoor swimming pool, elevator, security system, and a great deal of required maintenance. It was custom built for the Fowlers, who named it "Diamante." Vassos Dimitriou, the architect, was also the Honorary Consul for Crete. The design was beautiful, but a rectangular, flat roof, all-white exterior design would have been more suitable for a Greek island than for the Lake Washington shoreline.

Although the property had a southern exposure on a low, flat lot, nothing was done to protect the house from strong winds and rain. When it rains in the Seattle area, very often the weather comes up the lake from the south, carried by strong winds. Marvin Windows supplied seventy windows, which had no eaves, overhangs, awnings, or other protection from the wind-driven rain. Construction was completed in 1991, and not long after moving in, the Fowlers found some of the windows leaked every time it rained.

In response to the Fowlers' complaints, Marvin Windows sent local representatives, home office representatives, and outside inspectors to see what was the problem causing the windows to leak. Diamante's seventy windows had been a large sale for Marvin Windows, and they did not want their product associated with a gigantic leaking house on Lake Washington. Eventually at the end of 1998, they replaced all seventy windows in the house. They repaired the dry rot in the framing that they found in the course of replacing the windows. And they assured the Fowlers there would be no more problems.

The Fowlers had moved here from Hawaii and before that they had lived in Hong Kong. They couldn't get used to the damp drizzling Pacific Northwest weather. A year or so after replacing all the windows, they decided to put the house up for sale. This very large waterfront property was set for sale at a price few people could afford.

ᴧ ᴧ ᴧ

They buyers were among that group who could afford such a home, and during one visit the buyers brought along a *Wall Street Journal* reporter who was doing a story on the newly mega-rich in our area. The Internet boom was in full flower, and a smart guy with a new idea for a web site or a software product could become a dot-com multi-millionaire in the blink of an eye. The buyer had worked in the information technology world ever since emigrating to the U.S. from India where he graduated from a prestigious technical school. He made his first multimillion dollars at Microsoft. Then he left Microsoft and started a company with an idea that took off. Six months before the Fowlers decided to sell their home, the new company went public and its value skyrocketed. The buyers were ready to show the world they were right up there with Bill Gates.

During another visit, Mr. Fowler showed them around the house and he told them of the various maintenance issues associated with this large home and property, referring to a long list of contractors who were called in from time to time. The Mrs. asked questions and took notes diligently. Shortly into the walk-through, her husband's patience had run its course. Turning to his inquisitive wife, he said, "Shut up. I don't care about any of this. You are wasting my time." Mr. Fowler said she burst into tears and ran from the house. The walk-through was over.

I knew then and there that if this episode came into evidence at trial, and we had an all-woman jury, then the rest of the facts mattered little because we would likely prevail. Jurors pass judgment on people as much or more sometimes then the facts of the case, and if the jury does not like the plaintiff, then the facts of the case or the strength of the law must be overwhelming before the jury will be sympathetic to the plaintiff's case. As I saw it, an all women jury were not going to like the way this man treated his wife in front of others.

λ λ λ

During one of the visits to the property, Mr. Fowler told the buyer that all the windows had been replaced and there were some spare parts for them, but Mr. Fowler reported that he didn't seem to care. I believe they liked the fact that Diamante was just down the lake from Bill and Melinda Gates's new 66,000-square-foot home. Of course, during his trial testimony, he said they were quite happy with their modest rambler in Redmond.

Mr. Fowler's wife, Louvette, handled most of the negotiations over the price. She was born in the Philippines. The child of Chinese and Philippine parents, her father was an architect in Manila. Richard met Louvette when his fish cannery was a sponsor for a beauty pageant and she represented the Philippines. That year the Miss Universe pageant was set to take place in Lagos, Nigeria. When the Muslims complained about the prospect of women in bathing suits walking across the stage, the contest was moved to London. Louvette won the talent competition. By the time I met her, she had been a runway model, children's book author, photographer, and recording artist.

Louvette was appalled that this man brought a reporter into her home without the courtesy of asking first. It felt like a violation. Nevertheless, she was determined to be a courteous host, and in the British style of hospitality, she set a tea. The buyer, however, was not interested in her tea. In the end they settled on the price at $12,999,999. She told me thirteen was an unlucky number.

⋏ ⋏ ⋏

After they moved into their large Lake Washington waterfront home, the buyers began to make some improvements. In the process, they discovered dry rot in the framing, left over from the leaking windows. Apparently, the Marvin Windows' installers did not find all the dry rot when they replaced the windows. Believing they had been deceived in the sale, they filed suit against the Fowlers, Marvin Windows, and the realtor who handled the sale.

After I was retained, I went to look at the property. I could tell right away that the damages were going to be substantial. The house was covered in plastic, like a chrysalis, with scaffolding beneath the plastic sheathing. Clearly, this was going to be a very expensive repair job.

⋏ ⋏ ⋏

When I took the buyers' depositions, they both denied that the episode when he told her to shut up had ever occurred. No, nothing even remotely like that happened, they said. As soon as that walk-through was over, Mr. Fowler immediately called his real estate agent and told him the story. I used the doctrine of *res gestae* to get the realtor's account of what happened into evidence. Under the rules of evidence, *res gestae* is an exception to the hearsay rule.

Hearsay is testimony about something somebody other than the witness said out of court. According to the hearsay rule, hearsay offered to prove the truth of the matter contained in an alleged statement is not admissible evidence. They denied he said such things, and I wanted some corroboration of Mr.

Fowler's testimony about it. Besides, it would be helpful to tell that story from two different witnesses. The realtor's report of what Mr. Fowler had told him was classic hearsay. In fact, it was hearsay within hearsay because he was reporting what Mr. Fowler said the buyer had said. But one of the exceptions to the hearsay rule says that excited utterances relating to a startling event may be admissible when they are made under stress caused by the event.

This story, if it came into evidence, would be damaging to the plaintiffs' case. It was relevant to show the lack of reliance on any representations made by the seller. And it was not going to go over very well with an all-woman jury.

Before trial began, the plaintiffs filed a motion *in limine* to exclude the evidence arguing, not unreasonably, that it would be unfairly prejudicial. Our trial judge, Judge Terry Lukens, ruled, "Plaintiff alleges fraud, and one element of fraud is reliance on the statements the defendant made. Plaintiffs say they never said such a thing. The credibility of the witnesses is at issue; therefore, the evidence will be admitted."

人 人 人

Plaintiffs' attorney took the Fowlers' depositions, and the testimony was recorded on video. Naturally, wanting to look her best on camera, Louvette wore a spectacular outfit. She is a beautiful woman and had on what looked to me like a very expensive silk blouse, a pearl necklace and an aquamarine pants suit. She looked like a million bucks. That might be a problem with a King County jury, especially one of women only. I asked her to dress down – just a little – for trial.

⅄ ⅄ ⅄

Our defense theory on the fraud claim was that the Fowlers did not commit fraud because they did not knowingly make any false statements of fact that the buyers relied on. There are nine elements to a claim of fraud, each of which must be proven by "clear and convincing evidence." That is the highest standard of proof in a civil case, right below "reasonable doubt," which applies only in criminal cases. We focused our attention on two elements of the fraud case: the absence of any intentional deceit, and the lack of any evidence that the buyers relied on anything the Fowlers said in negotiating the sale.

The breach of contract case arose from the sale contract, which contained a disclosure statement with the question, "Are there presently any defects in the property?" The Fowlers checked the box "no" because Marvin Windows informed them that all the defects had been repaired.

The claim of negligence required proof of the lack of ordinary care, and our defense was that the Fowlers had always exercised care in the maintenance of their beautiful home and in speaking to the buyers about the house.

We spent a day in a mandatory mediation, where we tried without success to settle the case. At the end of the session, the mediator told me we were making a big mistake because we would lose at trial. He was wrong.

⅄ ⅄ ⅄

In preparing for trial, I was concerned about how to present Ms. Fowler. She was so beautiful and had something of an aristocratic air about her that might not sit well with a middle-class jury. We had photos used in marketing the property that showed its regal beauty, and my plan was to have her testify about the home in a Jackie Kennedy style White House home tour. I called one of their friends, Jeri Rice, to talk about whether she would testify to the home's exceptional maintenance, and I asked for her advice on how to present Ms. Fowler. She warned me against my plan and came to my office the next day to talk about it.

Jeri said she had seen how women in Bellevue reacted negatively to Ms. Fowler. Usually they were jealous and petty, but then again most of them were not as beautiful or privileged as Ms. Fowler. Jeri recommended that I ask Ms. Fowler to speak about her children instead of her home. They had three boys and the youngest was Ryan, her angel.

When I prepared the Fowlers for their testimony, I told Ms. Fowler if I thought she was putting on airs I would mention Ryan. That was going to be our code word. When I said "Ryan," she was supposed to settle down. It worked in way I never dreamed of.

Ms. Fowler's attire at trial was completely changed from what she wore at her deposition. I don't recall if she wore a skirt or dress or slacks, but she did wear a beautiful sweater with a high neck. It was a demure outfit – too demure if you knew her. Of course, the jury had just met her.

人 人 人

During jury selection, plaintiff's attorneys used their last peremptory challenge to remove the last man in the jury box. After the jury was seated and sworn in, I heard someone at their table say, "Look at that, we have an all-woman jury." As one of my favorite Marines, Gomer Pyle, used to say, "Surprise, surprise."

ʎ ʎ ʎ

When presenting a witness's testimony at trial, I usually don't like to work from a script of questions and answers. And I don't prepare my witnesses as if we were working from a script. Whether he or she is a client or lay witness, I will tell the witness the general topics that I plan to discuss with them. I tell them to keep their answers as short as they can and remain truthful. If I want more information, I'll ask another question. If there is a sore spot in the case or something in an email or other document that could be used against the witness, we'll review it so the witness knows what is coming and uses words that don't add fuel to the fire. But I believe the testimony will be more readily believed if it appears there is some spontaneity about the testimony. It is better to work through an issue than at it. When you speak from the heart and not a script, you convey the impression that you believe in what you say.

This approach can be scary at times. You might forget something. Lou Orland told us in law school there are always three arguments: what you planned to say, what you said, and what you thought you should have said later that night. Plus, you need to be quick on your feet if the witness says something you did not anticipate. I think that maxim applies to my sometimes impromptu technique in court.

In preparing for her deposition and the trial cross examination, we reviewed three keys to effective testimony. The first key is called active listening. The witness must listen to the question, and pay attention only to the question, not other distracting things like what the witness just said or what happened at breakfast or what is going to happen tonight or the lawyer's tie.

In a deposition in another case the witness was an attractive and very well turned out single woman. She was listening intently to the questions, or so I thought, when I noticed that the plaintiff's attorney, a regular Lothario, had acquired a leering look. He took on a wolf-like appearance and was nearly panting, and she was smiling back at him as an eager woman might. When I noticed what was happening, we took a break and I took the witness into my office and asked her, "what the hell were you doing in there?" She said, "I was just having a little fun." I put a stop to the fun. That is not what I call active listening.

The second key is to consider the response to ensure it is an answer to the question that was asked and not some other question. The third key is to deliver the response confidently, sitting with your hands in your lap away from your face or hair, and looking at the questioner directly.

⅄ ⅄ ⅄

I began my direct examination of Ms. Fowler by asking her to state her full name for the record. I like to stand at the far edge of the jury box so the jury can hear the witness and she can easily look toward the jury when she wants to. If you can avoid it, never examine a witness so that their back or side is facing the jury.

She said, "My name is Lourdes Louvette Visitacion Fowler." The court reporter had trouble with all of it and asked her to repeat it and to spell "Visitacion."

I said, "That is a very beautiful name."

She said, "Thank you, Mr. Bond."

I asked, "Where did your name come from?" I did not know I was going to ask that question until it came out of my mouth.

She said, "My father was a very religious man, and he wanted to honor Our Lady of Lourdes." I began to think I should leave this topic as quickly as possible.

In rapid sequence I used leading questions to establish that she grew up in the Philippines, worked as a runway model, recording artist, photographer, and children's book author and once was a beauty pageant winner. This part of her testimony I had planned and reviewed with Ms. Fowler in advance. I wanted the statement of her many accomplishments and successes to come from me and not from her. All she had to say was "yes," modestly.

We proceeded into the gist of the case, and I asked her about building this home, the problems with the windows, the assurances that the Marvin Windows workers gave them, the sale, and the utter surprise and dismay when the buyers sued them for fraud. At intermittent points along the way, I asked about her three boys. She loved to talk about her sons.

It never became necessary to execute my plan to use "Ryan" as a code word because she never did start to put on airs. About the second time I mentioned the name of one of her sons, I noticed that something interesting happened to her. When she spoke about one of her sons, she oozed a mother's love from every pore of her body.

We would talk about the windows, and I would ask, "What does Richard do for a living?" and the love would shine like a warm sunny day. We would talk about the sale process and I would ask, "How far did Robert go in school?" and the room warmed up again. Whenever I asked about Ryan, especially, the court room filled with the most amazing and soothingly warm mother's love imaginable. It was dramatic. Her friend Jeri was right. She loved her boys and it showed whenever she spoke about them.

We did this several more times, the same thing happened every time, and then I gave her over for cross-examination.

She handled every one of the questions on cross examination without a hitch. When plaintiffs' lawyer attempted to impeach her testimony with things she said in her deposition, he shot himself in the foot. In fact, he shot both of his feet. They used a TV monitor to show the video testimony, and they inserted the text from her deposition transcript at the bottom of the screen. The problem is they didn't show the text of all the answer she gave to the question. I noticed this the first time they played an excerpt from the video.

I interrupted them and complained loudly to the judge that they have to show all or none of the answer. Under the civil rules they could not use only portions of her deposition answer. The judge agreed with my objection and ordered them to read all of the answer she gave in the deposition. Undeterred by this error of judgment, they did it two more times, and each time I grew increasingly disgusted in my objections.

Plaintiff's lawyers lost considerable credibility with this little stunt. But to give credit where credit is due, the video clips also showed the jury brief glimpses of how Ms. Fowler looked when she dressed up. And that is all we needed because she looked terrific on the video.

When they finished the cross-examination, the judge looked at me and asked me if I had any more questions. I looked through my notes, shuffled the papers, and pretended to think for a minute. Then I looked up and asked, "Ms. Fowler, did I ask you about Ryan?"

A Niagara Falls of love poured out of her even though she didn't say a word. The all-woman jury giggled in delightful pleasure. Judge Lukins blushed. My heart was pounding so loud I was afraid someone might hear it. That question, which was admittedly calculated and yet completely unplanned, cemented the jurors' affection for Ms. Fowler. They loved her. After the trial, two of the jurors asked me where they might purchase her children's books.

$$\lambda \quad \lambda \quad \lambda$$

The cross-examination of Mr. Buyer was almost as spontaneous and almost as much fun. He is a brilliant man who was used to being the one in charge, and he wrestled with me over nearly every question. A front-page article from the *Wall Street Journal* about his visit to the Fowler property came in handy.

My objective was to show that he did not rely on anything the Fowlers had said in the course of the sale. I figured one way to demonstrate a lack of reliance was by showing a determined intent to buy the largest, most expensive house on Lake Washington, just down the waterfront from the mansion Bill and Melinda Gates had built. Although they were already well off, they were suddenly very wealthy from the IPO of his new company, and maybe I could show that money was burning a hole in their pockets. He denied all those motives. In the course of his time on the stand, some helpful testimony came in.

I asked, "When you purchased the house, your net worth was in excess of $100 million; isn't that right?" I thought this question might draw an objection. Ordinarily a party's financial status is not relevant. In most cases, counsel will file a motion in limine before trial to exclude any reference to the wealth or poverty of the client. Here my question drew no objection, by then it was probably too late.

He replied, "I'm not sure – quite sure. When you say 'net worth,' you mean the money that we had? No, we did not have that money. You know."

I said, "The value of your estate, the actual value of all your holdings, the value of all of your property was in excess of $100 million. Isn't that right?"

He replied, "That depends on the – where the stock rise price on it that particular day would have been. So they go up and down every day, every second."

Wondering out loud, I asked, "Did it go up above two or three billion?" The court reporter took it down as million, but my question was billion with a "B."

He said, "It went up to seven billion at one point." Again, the transcript incorrectly said "million."

I looked at the jury and with an incredulous and wondrous tone of voice asked, "Seven billion dollars?"

He said, "I think so."

A few minutes later, I asked, "right before the realtor presented the house to you, you had sold a large block of stock for two hundred million or more; isn't that right?"

He said, "I don't – you mean I don't – yes, we did sell some stock in the secondary offering. But numbers – number seems higher than what I remember. But it could be."

I asked the clerk to mark the *Wall Street Journal's* front page article about the sale of the house, and I handed it to the witness and asked, "Does that report refresh your memory that you had recently sold stock to collect two hundred million in cash?"

He replied, "Says about two hundred. And I'm just saying after tax, it would have been lot less is what – that's what I was trying to say. I wasn't denying or anything."

⅄ ⅄ ⅄

The courtroom visitors usually are elderly folks who come down to watch whatever is happening that day. By the end of this trial our usual visitors were joined by lawyers and others who heard something interesting was happening in Judge Lukens' courtroom. It was David and Goliath. Plaintiffs had three lawyers and two paralegals at counsel table. I prefer to try cases by myself. The odds were five to one. My wife told me later I had them outnumbered. In my summation I told the jury they were fortunate to get to hear the "Case of the Billionaire versus the Millionaire."

During jury deliberations I asked Mr. Fowler to take a seat in the hallway right outside the court room. I instructed him to sit there when the jurors came and went and look as forlornly as he could muster. At one point there was a dust up when one of the jurors brought in a dictionary to look up a word.

After all the parties and lawyers had assembled, the jury entered the court room and took their seats in the jury box. The courtroom was packed with observers, every seat was taken and others stood in the doorway. It reminded me of my second argument in the Washington Supreme Court, a case called *Keytronic vs. Aetna*. A pollution insurance coverage case, with over 25 *Amicus* Briefs, national attention and, at oral argument, a standing room only crowd of lawyers in what is a very large courtroom at the Temple of Justice in Olympia. As I was sitting at counsel table rehearsing my argument, I began to look around for the trash can in case I needed to throw up. And then I decided it would be better if I didn't know where it was as a means of preventing me from throwing up. With time, those nerves ceased getting so riled up. But going down to take a verdict is always exciting. Did we win or lose, and if it's a loss, how bad will it be?

⅄ ⅄ ⅄

The clerk in the *David vs. Goliath* battle read the verdict. "Did the defendants commit fraud?"

The answer was "no," and I thought, good that solves the insurance coverage problem. My clients had insurance, but not if there was fraud.

"Did the defendants breach the contract?"

Again, the answer was "no." I liked the direction this was heading.

"Were the defendants negligent?"

The answer to that question also was "no." There were no other questions to answer.

At that moment, the courtroom erupted in pandemonium, reminding me of the final scene in the film *A Passage to India,* when the victim recants the allegation of rape in middle of the trial. Everybody started talking at once, loudly. I looked over at Mr. Fowler who was leaned back in his chair with his mouth gapping wide open in shock. I thought he might have a heart attack right there. I grabbed his arm and said, "Richard, you won!"

He looked at me with wide eyes and said, "No, Michael, you won!"

Somebody, not our side, had called the local newspaper and a reporter came to hear the verdict. As soon as the verdict was announced, plaintiff bolted from the court room without saying anything to anybody. I stayed for an interview and for the first of probably five or six times when the press covered one of my trials, the reporter quoted me correctly.

The sales contract provided for attorney fees and costs to the prevailing party and we received a substantial award of fees and costs when the judgment was entered. Plaintiffs appealed, and the verdict was upheld.

118

Chapter 7

The Motor Pool

Like a bad penny that keeps coming back, some claimants will keep you busy. Once at a conference in São Paulo, I met an English lawyer who worked in Cairo, Egypt; he told me about a hotel that was a "fountain of work" for him. First there was a construction claim, which was followed a few years later by an operations claim, and then the hotel partners fell out. This fountain-of-work hotel provided him with much good and lucrative work over the years. A small Tacoma contractor, whom I will call C&C, did the same for me.

The cases with C&C arose out of two school construction projects. The first case involved the construction of a new elementary school in the City of Orting. The site is located beside the Puyallup River, which flows off the Mt. Rainier watershed. The geology beneath Orting consists of what is known as the Electron Mudflow. Deposited by a lahar mudflow from an eruption of Mt. Rainier about 10,000 years ago, the soil is made up of deep volcanic debris that is very difficult to work in especially when it is wet. The water table is close to the surface. The soils and high water table at the site presented many challenges to the design and construction of the new school. The school district had no other choice for the site. They had to have another elementary school and all of the Orting geology is consists of the Electron Mudflow.

The civil engineers added several features to the construction documents to address the site's soil and water issues. C&C ignored almost every one of these design measures, all of which were intended to help them deal with the geological challenges of the site. During construction, mud and debris flowed off the construction site causing the City inspectors to issue citations and fines for failure to comply with the approved plans. The contractor dug large holes, ran pumps all day to drain the holes, and then turned the pumps off at night. The next morning they returned to the project to find several deep ponds where they needed to build. The site flooded and the contractors literally got stuck in the mud.

Well before the construction work was completed, C&C asserted a claim against the school district alleging that the design documents were negligently drawn and that the designer's negligence was the cause of all their trouble on the project. The district's attorneys informally denied the claim. Then the contractor filed suit against the school district. The district's attorneys denied the claim and argued that the contractor was responsible for the problems resulting from the failure to adhere to the plans. The suit lay dormant for several months.

The contracts were in the traditional design-bid-build arrangement. The owner hired an architect who then hired the engineers. When the plans were completed, the owner asked contractors to submit bids, and C&C were the low bidders. On public works contracts, the owner is required as a general rule to accept the lowest responsive bid from a responsible contractor. Under this traditional contractual arrangement, there are two lines of contract, one between the owner and the designers and the second between the owner and the contractor. There is no contract between the contractor and the designers, and the lack of privity of contract usually prevents the contractor from suing the designers directly.

The claim percolated for several months and then the school district asked the architect to respond. The architect said the contractor was solely at fault, and so the district sued the architect. The district alleged that if the contractor's assertions that the design was bad were true, then the architect should defend the district and indemnify them for any award. The claim percolated some more, and after a while the architect asked the civil engineer to respond. I was retained to defend the civil engineer, and we said the contractor was solely at fault. The architect then sued the civil engineer. They alleged the claims all arose from the engineer's design for the site and if the design was bad, then the engineer should pay for any damages the contractor could prove.

Beyond answering the complaints, including the third-party complaint against the architect and the fourth-party complaint against the engineer, nobody did anything more about the suit until we attended a mediation of the claims.

My client, the civil engineer, was very unhappy that he was being blamed for the problems the contractor had on the site. His project engineer, Cynthia, a very competent and careful woman, had overseen the design for the site to ensure that it dealt adequately with the poor soils and high water table. If the contractor had followed the work measures called out in the civil design documents for the site rather than ignoring them, they probably would have had no trouble.

Most professionals are insured for professional liability claims under insurance policies that require the consent of the professional when a settlement is proposed. The idea, I guess, is to prevent the insurer from buying out of a claim that might impact the professional's reputation. Often, these "consent to settle" policies inject a fluid dynamic to the resolution of the claim. Fluid is probably the wrong expression. It can be more like an immovable stone wall – and in this case my engineer was an immovable stone wall.

At the mediation, the mediator tried in vain to persuade him to offer something, anything, to extricate his firm from the claim. After all, everybody else was going to offer something. The school district and the architect wanted to settle. Of course, they were both represented by very high-priced lawyers, while I worked for the bargain basement insurance company rate.

My view of the case was that if we took it to a jury, nine times out of ten we would win, but I knew there were tangible and intangible costs involved in demanding one's day in court. I explained all of these costs to the client, and he said "not one red cent" was to be paid in settlement.

Most of the case settled in the mediation. The school district paid a little money and assigned its rights to sue architect to the contractor. The architect's insurance company also paid a little money and assigned its rights to sue the civil engineer to the school district and contractor. And the engineer, who was left holding the bag, held firm to his position that he would not consent to pay "one red cent."

His insurance company threw us a curve ball a few months before trial. My client's contract with the architect included a prevailing party clause for attorney fees, which meant if we won the case, we would recover the attorney fees. Of course, it also meant that if we lost, we would have to pay the other side's attorney fees. The insurance company took the position that this was a contractual liability that was not covered under the insurance policy. They said, "Sorry, but we won't pay any attorney fee award."

I thought it was a little too late to play that card and referred the client to a local lawyer who specialized in suing insurance companies on behalf of the policy holder. I could have handled the issue myself, but that insurance company sent me a lot of work. Threatening to sue them would not go over well with the folks who decide where to send the work. Besides, it's just more effective to bring in an outside coverage counsel. He succeeded in persuading the insurance company to back off its new argument, and we prepared for trial.

ᚠ ᚠ ᚠ

The juries in this county had improved in the twenty-plus years I'd been trying cases in that court house. When I started, we had a blue-collar jury pool with many elderly and retired folks. It used to be that we did not encounter many highly educated folks or business owners. But over time, the county demographics changed. Now the jury pool included software engineers, airline pilots, folks who owned their own business, in addition to men or women who worked on the waterfront or on an assembly line. It is much easier these days to select a jury that is more likely to be skeptical of damage claims.

As the trial progressed, things began to look increasingly positive. I was pleased with the jury we assembled, which was 50 percent female and included a good-looking flight attendant in the back row. My project engineer, a woman, was a key witness and I figured she would play well as a woman working in the male-dominated field of engineering and heavy construction. While I prefer to try cases alone, this was my third multi-week trial that year, so I asked an associate, Ray, to help out. I was glad he was there.

The contractors were helpful, too, in their own way. One of them came to court dressed in Bermuda shorts, a Hawaiian shirt and flip flops. I couldn't believe my eyes when I saw him. Dressing that way was very disrespectful of the court and jury, who were not there as volunteers. He proved to be an arrogant jerk on the stand, and his partner's demeanor on the stand was even more arrogant. After I had finished my cross-examination, I turned to walk back to counsel table.

When I sat down Ray leaned over and said, "When your back was to him, he made eye contact with the flight attendant and winked at her."

I whispered, "Perfect!" I was confident he had done nothing to ingratiate himself with her, the opposite was true. Several of the jurors no doubt saw it, too, and would be similarly unimpressed. Sometimes they hand it up to you on a silver platter.

It was closing in on the time when my project engineer would testify. She had been raised by a single father, who was an engineer. She dressed the way I imagined her father had dressed, in well-worn jeans, work boots, and flannel shirts. She was married to a good man, and it seemed to me that she probably did not have much in the way of pretty things as a girl growing up. I wanted to soften her appearance for the jury. The Friday before she was to appear in court, I asked the client's wife if she would take Cynthia shopping over the weekend to buy a pink, silk blouse for her appearance in court. She said she would be happy to do what I asked.

On Monday morning, I met up with Cynthia in the hallway outside the court room. She was wearing a new blue suit with coat and trousers and an orange shirt. I said, "It looks like you went shopping over the weekend."

She said, "Yes, I did." I didn't know if she knew what I had been up to.

I asked, "Where did you go?"

She replied, "Men's Warehouse."

To paraphrase the saying, "You can take the woman out of the country, but you can't take the country out of the woman."

She had purchased a man's blue suit. I told her it looked very nice, but I asked her to take the coat off and leave it in her car.

As I was presenting Cynthia's testimony, I began to notice her new orange shirt more closely. I looked down at my own shirt to confirm where the buttons were. For reasons that I never knew, women's shirts are sewn with the buttons on the other side. She was wearing a man's shirt. Smiling inside at my foolish plan, I realized she wasn't going to do what *this* man wanted, even if I was her lawyer.

After all the testimony was in, the trial judge agreed with me on all the jury instructions. In order to prove a case, first the contractor would have to prove it was entitled to compensation under its contract with the owner. If they got over that hurdle, then they would have to prove the architectural firm breached its contract with the owner. And only if they overcame that hurdle, then they would have to prove the civil engineer was liable to the architect under their contract.

It helped that the school district's superintendent came in and testified that she was very happy with the architect. The architect, a man named Tizzy, came in and testified that he saw no problem with the engineer's performance.

In final argument I played a woman's plight to the hilt. Not only do they do all the things that make our lives livable, things that in many cases we men could do ourselves if we got off our lazy butts once in a while. But when they work in a male-dominated field, such as engineering or construction, they have to work much harder than the men just to have any hope of staying employed, let alone getting paid comparably for the work. In this particular project, I argued Cynthia went out of her way in completing the drawings to make it easy for this contractor to get in and out of this job and make a profit. And after I worked myself up into something of a fevered pitch, I looked over at the flight attendant and concluded by asking, "What more did this woman have to do to make these men happy?" She nodded as if to say she knew exactly what I was getting at.

It takes about thirty minutes to drive from the court house to my office and I headed to my office after the case was submitted to the jury. When I got to my office, my secretary told me the jury had a verdict. I took the verdict by telephone. It was twelve to zero for the defense.

⅄ ⅄ ⅄

C&C came back to give me another case several years later. This one concerned the renovation of a swimming pool and associated locker rooms for a local high school. The contractor ran into trouble with lead paint that had to be removed in the renovation, and then the sealant used in the pool failed. These events and others caused delay, and C&C again said it was all the fault of the architect's bad design or misleading drawings or ambiguous answers to questions. The creative excuses never cease to amaze me. As before, every one of the contractor's problems was the result of his failure to follow the requirements of the contract drawings and specifications.

I caught wind of the claim when the architect, a long time client, called me to ask for help in responding to these accusations. I contacted the school district's attorney, whom I had known for many years. He told me the district was going to make an offer of settlement of $200,000, and the contractor's lawyer said they would probably accept the $200,000 offer if the district assigned its rights to sue the architect. I told the district's attorney I had been down this path with this contractor once before.

I suggested that if the district would pay the architect the $200,000 it was willing to spend, then the architect could take over the case and defend the school district. We worked out a deal along those lines and I took over the defense of the case. The district agreed to pay the architect $50,000 and they would hold $150,000 in reserve for settlement if the opportunity arose.

Once I had taken over the case, we offered to settle all claims for $150,000. That offer was rejected. C&C demanded $750,000.

ᴧ ᴧ ᴧ

I needed an expert witness for the sealant that was failing in the swimming pool, among other issues. I contacted a local forensic engineering firm I use from time to time and they referred me to the in-house sealant expert. He sent me his resume. While he had education and experience evaluating sealants in various uses, including uses under water, the resume he sent me showed that his first fifteen years of employment was with the U.S. Army where he was assigned to the Motor Pool. I'm not sure if he thought this pool experience was relevant to the case I called about, but I decided we would not need a sealant expert after all. From then on Marianne and I referred to this case as "the Motor Pool case."

The architects and I worked up a long list of the various portions of the contract and specifications that C&C appeared to ignore during the project. These failures to perform could be considered conditions of the contract. C&C had sued the District for breach of contract. As one of the elements of a claim for breach of contract, C&C would have to prove that it complied with all conditions of the contract. For example, the lead paint specifications required that they submit a work plan showing how they intended to ensure a safe work place when lead dust was created. They failed to submit any plan and proceeded to sand blast the lead paint with no protective measures, and the architect issued a stop work order when he saw what they were doing. Among other things, C&C alleged the stop work order caused them delay damages.

The civil rules say the answer to the complaint must allege a failure of conditions precedent with specificity if the defendant intends to assert that issue as an affirmative defense. The School District's attorney filed the answer to the complaint before I took over the case, and it did not specifically allege there was a failure of conditions precedent or what those conditions were. As good luck would have it, I reviewed the answer to see if this issue had been taken care of when I saw that our pleadings were not complete. So, I prepared a motion to amend the answer to set out each of the conditions of the contract that C&C had failed to fulfill.

C&C's lawyer opposed the motion. She argued that we were too late. She said the case was pending for over a year, the trial was set for only a few months away, and we had conducted too much discovery with depositions and interrogatories to permit new theories of the case to be injected at this late date.

The morning of our hearing the court room was full of lawyers arguing their motions. I had never been in this judge's court before, but he looked familiar. He was tough on the lawyers who were up to argue their cases before my motion was called. I was bracing for a difficult hearing because I was asking for a major change in the pleadings on the eve of trial.

Before we began to argue the motion to amend, the judge looked at me and made a disclosure.

He said, "Counsel, I need to disclose that Mr. Bond and I were law school class mates."

I said, "Your honor looked familiar but I couldn't place you."

He said, "You were one of three of us who went on to serve our country after graduation from law school."

That is an interesting, old-school, way to put it, and it signaled a comradeship that might serve me and my client well. I said, "Yes, your honor, I became a Marine Corps Judge Advocate."

He said, "Yes, I know. I became a Judge Advocate in the US Army." He had a long memory as this was over 30 years ago. We had not seen each other since then, and I still don't recall ever meeting.

Then he looked at C&C's lawyer to see if she had anything she wanted to say. If it had been me, I think I would have considered asking the judge to recuse himself. In our state each side gets one chance to change the judge before he makes a discretionary ruling, and she could have exercised that chance right then and there. She thanked the judge for making the disclosure and said she had nothing to add.

The right to change the judge in our state is akin to the peremptory challenge of a prospective juror in a jury trial. No reason must be given and it is reversible error if the judge denies the request to recuse him or herself. In the right case the trial lawyer may ask for the right to *voir dire* the judge, especially where the judge has made a disclosure like he did in this case. For example, C&C's lawyer might have asked him if he had any contact with me since law school or if we belonged to the same bar groups or community organizations or church. That might have prompted the judge to tell us that he was active in Rotary with the school district's assistant superintendent and one of my architects both of whom were certain to be witnesses at the trial.

The defense used *voir dire* on a judge in one of my Marine Corps trials. Following a fatal accident on an aircraft carrier, every person in the Navy and Marine Corps was ordered to submit to urinalysis, and I was assigned to prosecute the first case in San Diego arising from a failed urine test. We caught wind that all the judges had attended a meeting with the Commanding Officer of the judges to discuss how they were going to handle these urinalysis cases. The defense was interested in knowing whether things said at this meeting would provide grounds for a claim of unlawful command influence. After inquiring of the judge, who granted the defense request for *voir dire*, they found no grounds for a challenge. But the lesson is, don't shy away from asking the judge a few questions if he or she gives you the chance.

Our motion to amend the answer was granted and the judge gave C&C a continuance of the trial date for as long as she wanted. The case settled about three weeks later for $60,000.

Chapter 8

Illustrative Exhibits

A jury trial can be a very boring affair for jurors. After the first excitement of coming down to court in response to the summons and being herded in and out of courtrooms until they finally make it onto a jury, the trial itself is typically punctuated with boring intermissions when either nothing of much interest happens or the lawyers and judges expound at length about obscure subjects. The testimony of witnesses unused to public speaking may be just as hard to follow. A day in court can be mentally fatiguing, with afternoons dragging on. The skilled trial lawyer will try to liven up the process.

When I first came to Seattle, Tom Lee of the Lee Smart firm told us that if a witness is doing major damage to your case, then try "accidentally" knocking over the water pitcher that sits on counsel table to distract the jury. I never tried that one though there have been times when such a distraction would have been useful. Instead of resorting to such a messy tactic, I found I could effectively gain the jury's attention with interesting illustrative exhibits. Here are four examples of illustrative exhibits I used to keep the jury's attention and sell my case.

ᚠ ᚠ ᚠ

In the *MacDonald* asbestos case I described in A Product Liability, the medical issues played a large role in the win. Asbestosis is a lung disease, in the category of lung diseases called *pneumoconiosis,* or "dust disease of the lungs." At that time there were two medical tests that the doctors typically used to examine for and diagnose asbestosis. One test evaluated how well the lungs performed in getting the air in and out of the lungs, where the oxygen would pass from the lungs into the blood stream. We used Dr. Smith to address that evidence.

Another test examined the patient's chest x-ray. Qualified radiologists could look at the x-ray and diagnose asbestosis, based on certain unique characteristics shown on the x-ray film. In the early stages of the asbestos litigation, the three features on x-ray that I recall were used were:

1. blunting of the costophrenic angle,
2. diffuse irregular opacities or spots throughout the lung field, usually concentrated in the lower lungs, and
3. calcified plaques.

The costophrenic angle is at the bottom of the lung cavity, turning down at a thirty-degree angle where the diaphragm meets the edge of the body. When it is "blunted," the disease process obscures that angle from view. The diffuse opacities or spots are distinctive in the lung field, and the calcified plaques show up on the x-ray as bright white blobs often on the diaphragm.

The presence of these findings is based on a comparison of the patient's x-ray with the standard films produced by International Labor Organization's (ILO) International Classification of Radiographs of pneumoconiosis. The ILO standard films came in a full range of the disease process. A person trained in reading chest x-rays would compare the patient's chest x-ray to the standard films and make a partial diagnosis from that comparison. A film showing no disease was labeled 0/0. The films labeled 1/1, 2/2 or 3/3 showed increasing disease, with 3/3 being the most advanced stage of very severe lung disease. We had a set of the standard films in our office.

One of the oddities about Mr. McDonald's condition was that his chest x-ray looked like the 0/0 ILO standard film.

Plaintiffs called an eminent physician from the Mt. Sinai Medical Center in New York and he testified that in his considered medical opinion Mr. McDonald had a classic case of asbestosis. I used the ILO standard films to try to cast doubt on his conclusion.

We retrieved every light box used to show x-rays in the courthouse. Light boxes are usually used to show things like broken bones in car crash cases. I set up four light boxes in front of the jury and we dimmed the lights slightly. I put the 3/3 standard film on the box and asked the witness to tell the jury what the ILO standard films are and how they are used in practice. He explained that a specialist in reading chest x-rays would compare the patient's chest x-ray to the standard films and make a diagnosis by comparing the two x-rays. It was important for the jury to know these were used outside of a litigation context. The doctor assured the jury that these were reliable sources of information. I asked him about the various features shown on the 3/3 film. You could readily see the diffuse irregular opacities concentrated in the lower lungs, the completely blunted costophrenic angle, and the dramatic presentation of calcified plaques. That poor guy had a bad case of disabling asbestosis.

Leaving the 3/3 film on its light box, I put the 2/2 film up next to it. We talked about the three characteristic features of advanced lung disease. In this film, all three features were present, though not as dramatically evident. Then I put the 1/1 film next to the 2/2 film. The jury began to sit up and lean forward to try to see the evidence of lung disease the doctor from Mt. Sinai described. At this point it appeared that the jury was almost ready to make their own diagnosis as radiologists. Then I put up the 0/0 film and everyone could see that the man had no lung disease at all, let alone the disabling lung disease called asbestosis.

Leaving all four films on their light boxes, I put up Mr. MacDonald's most recent x-ray before he had died. The jury's reaction was spontaneous and visible. His film showed none of the features used to make the diagnosis. His x-ray was as clear if not clearer than the 0/0 standard film.

The witness had sworn that, based upon his examination of the patient's x-rays, Mr. MacDonald had a classic case of asbestosis, and we just demonstrated that his diagnosis could not possibly be correct.

I believe this demonstration cleared the way for the jury ultimately to render a verdict in favor of the defense. After two months of trial and two and half days of final arguments, they began deliberating the case at three o'clock on a Friday afternoon. They told us the vote was immediately ten to two for the defense, but they wanted to give it the weekend so it didn't look so bad. Mr. MacDonald simply was not sick from asbestos.

ㅅ ㅅ ㅅ

In *Uplinger vs. Six Flags*, two men were working in the bucket of a boom lift at the Wild Waves Theme Park installing cable between two power poles when they contacted a high voltage power line. The operator of the boom lift was electrocuted and died almost instantly, and his co-worker was severely injured. The state investigator concluded that the men hit the power line while trying to lift the bucket up over a row of fir trees in order to string the new cable.

They were installing cable and working under a contract with my client, who was a telecommunications system supplier. My client was one of many defendants in the wrongful death and injury case, along with Six Flags who owned the park. The suit alleged my client was negligent for not ensuring the work site was safe in part, the theory went, because the tree tops were too close to the energized power lines.

As they did whenever a death occurs at a job site, the Washington State Department of Labor and Industries conducted an investigation and took dozens of photographs of the accident scene. Although the photographs showed a great deal, they proved to be inadequate. All the photographs were taken from the ground looking up, and they showed tree branches that seemed to grow up into the power lines. None of the photos taken in the investigation was shot from a position where you might see whether where they were trying to hang the new cable there was, in fact, any room between the top of the trees and the power lines.

The accident happened in 2007, and the plaintiffs filed the lawsuit over a year later.

I retained an electrical engineer with expertise in electrocution cases. In late 2010 he and I were in my office conference room working out a reconstruction of what the men were doing when they ran into the power line. The more we worked on it, the less likely it seemed that the trees had anything to do with the cause of the electrocution. Meanwhile, it became increasing clear to me that we needed to know exactly how tall the trees were on the date of accident, which was more than three years ago at that point. The information I needed turned out to be closer to home than I had imagined.

While talking about my interest in finding a tree expert, my electrical engineer expert told me his first degree was in forestry, and he spent his summers as a "cruiser" for a timber company. Cruisers hike through the forests and measure the height and circumference of the trees for the timber company. He went on to explain that a fir tree grows a new set of branches every year, which show up as the rings in the core of the tree. All you had to do was count the branches down from the most recent set of branches and then you would know how tall the tree was on the date in question. "I can tell you exactly how tall those trees were on the date of accident," he assured me.

I needed a photograph to tell the story. I recalled I had a surveyor client, Norm Larson, who had shown me a new instrument that used laser stations to shoot images of a feature. They set up the laser station, shot the images – as many as 500,000 images per minute – and then moved the station, eventually repeating the process at a dozen or more places all around the object. Next, they used a software program to combine the data from the scanning stations and create an image of the feature they were shooting. The first time Norm demonstrated this tool to me, he showed me an image of a Boeing 737 jetliner. I was impressed. It could have been a very high-definition photograph.

Norm sent a crew out to image the scene of the accident. After reconstructing the data into an image, he reduced the top of the trees by the distance of three years' growth, based on my forestry expert's information. The result was an image depicting the scene of the accident on the date it occurred. It showed a very large space between the tree tops and the power line, which could mean there was no good reason to have raised the boom lift as high as they did. The accident was nobody's fault other than the deceased fellow's poor judgment while operating the lift.

At Norm's deposition, the plaintiffs' attorney asked, "Is this your best estimate of what the scene looked like on the date of accident?"

"No, this is exactly what it looked like," Norm replied.

We negotiated a favorable settlement shortly thereafter.

人 人 人

Sometimes you have only one thing to say at trial and that was my predicament in *Broadview vs. Koll Construction*. So I said just that one thing over and over and over again, and we brought it to life with an illustrative exhibit.

My client was the design builder of a complex of five buildings used as a retirement home for retired school teachers. The complex was built during a boom of multifamily residential construction in our region, most of which leaked like sieves and all of these projects kept legions of construction lawyers busy in the ensuing construction defect litigation.

The litany of construction defects on these projects, including the retirement complex in my case, was amazing. Building paper was lapped the wrong way and funneled rain water that fell behind the siding into the wall framing. In some cases, they neglected to install any building paper at all. Deck and window sill framing was built with a slope into the building rather than away from the building, allowing rain water to flow into the units. Window and door flashing was either missing entirely or installed incorrectly. If you have not heard, it rains in Seattle, and this complex leaked from the date the first retired teacher moved in. The leaks allowed mold and mildew to grow.

By the time the owner hired an attorney, it was believed among construction lawyers that the six-year statute of limitations on a claim for repair of the defects had expired, and just barely. But then the court of appeals decided a case that resurrected this old claim and the owner filed suit.

The builder had undoubtedly failed to follow the plans and good industry practices, and there was no way to defend the case on those facts. If we could show that the owner knew or should have known by July 1996 that the leaks were caused by these construction defects, then the old statute of limitations would apply and bar the suit.

In many respects having only one issue greatly simplified the case. But I had to practice telling the jury with a straight face that even though my client built a giant pile of crap where all these retired school teachers lived, the owner just waited too long to file the suit.

人 人 人

We had a major setback before we got to trial. We had hired an associate attorney from New Orleans whose first assignment was to help me in discovery and motions practice. She was an outstanding litigator with significant trial experience in the New Orleans Parish prosecuting attorney's office. She was doing a great job, keeping the plaintiff's attorney back on his heels when, about six months after coming to work for us, she committed suicide. We learned later that she had significant trouble with drug and alcohol abuse and multiple hospitalizations while working in New Orleans. She was always well dressed and groomed. Our office manager took her mother and brother to the apartment to retrieve her personal belongings, and she reported back to us it was a miracle the woman was able to wear two of the same shoes every day. The lesson there is to always check into new hires from out of state. We were so impressed with her interview that we didn't check into her past the way we should have.

ᴧ ᴧ ᴧ

In jury selection, all I had to work with was the statute of limitations. And so I asked the prospective jurors whether there might be any objections to a statute of limitations, and each one answered no. I asked them how the statute of limitations might be useful to a business person. After I asked the third juror what value he might see in a statute of limitations, the trial judge interrupted me and said, "Mr. Bond, can we have a sidebar here?"

"Yes, of course, Judge McBroom," I replied. What was I going to say? "Later judge. Can't you see I'm busy trying to brainwash this jury?"

When we went out into the hallway out of the hearing of the jury, Judge McBroom said, "Mr. Bond, I am not too sure what you are doing here, but (pointing at a loose-leaf binder he brought with him) it says here in my judge's handbook that the lawyers are not supposed to ask the jury if they agree with the law or not."

My opponent chimed in, "Yeah, you know I was just about to object to those questions."

The judge said, "Why don't you ask them something else?"

I said, "Yes, your honor."

ᴧ ᴧ ᴧ

I saved the illustrative exhibit for the last witness in the defense case; she was the owner of the retirement complex. The exhibit was mounted on a large foam-core board with a drawing of all five buildings in the complex. I had placed in evidence all of the maintenance slips kept by the maintenance staff of the complex. There were over a hundred of these slips, and all but a small handful were complaints of leaks. I divided the maintenance slips into four groups, in chronological order. If we could show that by July, 1996 the owner knew or should have known that the leaks were the result of construction defects, then the statute of limitations would bar the claim.

I went through the first group of maintenance requests for the time period up to July, 1993. I asked the witness to read off the date and unit number where the leak occurred, and I put a round orange sticker on the exhibit at the unit that was leaking. There were twenty-five or so orange dots on the exhibit when we finished.

I asked, "If you had known that your buildings were leaking like this as of July, 1993, do you believe you would have been on notice that you had a problem?"

She answered immediately and firmly, "No."

Then she identified the next group of complaints about leaks up through July, 1994, and the orange dots were beginning to multiply. I asked the question again. "If you had known your buildings were leaking like this as of July, 1994, do you think you would have been on notice that you had a problem?"

Less firmly this time she said, "I don't think so."

Then we did it again with the next group of complaints about leaks up through July, 1995, and I added more orange dots to the exhibit. I asked the question again. "If you had known your buildings were leaking like this as of July, 1995, do you think you would have been on notice that you had a problem?"

A bit more subdued this time, she said, "Maybe." I knew I had her right where I wanted her.

We did it one more time. When the complaints of leaks up to July, 1996 were shown with the orange dots on the exhibit, it looked like the complex of five buildings had come down with a bad case of chickenpox. I asked the question one more time. "If you had known your building was leaking like this as of July, 1996, do you think you would have been on notice that you had a problem?"

This time she fought back and protested, "I didn't know about this."

I was ready for that argument and said, "But these reports were prepared by your maintenance supervisor, right?"

"Yes, they were."

"And he was working within the course and scope of his duties – working for your organization, right?" The law of principle and agent says that the knowledge of an agent acquired in the course and scope of his employment by the principle is deemed to be knowledge of the principle.

"Yes, he was."

"If you had known your buildings were leaking like this as of July, 1996, do you think you would have been on notice that you had a problem?"

This time she looked down and in a whisper said, "Yes." And then one of those moments you only see on the old *Perry Mason* show happened.

One of the jurors hollered out, "We can't hear you, would you keep your voice up?"

She looked up and said for all to hear, "Yes."

I followed up. "And you would have hired an expert, like you did, and he would have informed you that the leaks were caused by the contractor's failure to build the project according to the plans or good practice?"

"That's right."

"And you would have known all of that before July, 1996?"

"Yes."

The next morning, plaintiff took our last offer and the case settled. The evidence was plain to see in all its orange glory, easily understood, and it led to only one conclusion. This complex for retired school teachers leaked badly, and it always had leaked. The owner should have done something about it long before she did.

᛭ ᛭ ᛭

Engineering drawings proved useful in *DBM vs. Sanders*. In this case, an engineering firm sued to collect fees they incurred for two short plat developments. The developer believed that he was being overcharged and refused to pay. The engineer filed a lien against the property, and when he sued on his contract and to foreclose his lien, the developer asserted a counterclaim for negligence, breach of contract, and fraud. I was retained to defend the counterclaim under the engineer's professional liability insurance policy. We took over the fee claim, too.

A short plat begins with a set of preliminary plans. When those are approved and after the developer completes the improvements, such as roads, curbs, gutters, sidewalks, and utilities, then the engineer must update the preliminary plans to show the as built conditions and record the final plat map showing all the improvements. Throughout the county's review process, the county reviewer keeps track of his or her time, which is billed to the developer.

The developer's attorney called the county reviewing official to testify, and they put all of his time records into evidence. He testified to the importance of keeping good time records. As he explained, if they fail to do so, they can get in trouble. And if they don't respond to a supervisor's warnings about keeping good time records, they can lose their jobs. Together the developer's lawyer and the county witness went through the county's time records, and they compared the county records with the engineer's invoices, which were similarly detailed, showing dates, places, persons present and the subjects of all meetings. In a dozen or more instances, the engineer invoiced time for a meeting with the reviewer whose own records showed no such meeting ever occurred. The developer's attorney had shown that there was no meeting or discussion of the project on the dates when the engineer had billed for such a meeting.

There wasn't much I could do on cross-examination of this witness.

We made up all this lost ground when the developer's expert witness testified. The expert, a professional engineer who had worked on many of these kinds of projects, took the final plat maps and compared them to the preliminary maps. He found a half dozen or so changes on both short plat maps, and his opinion was that the billings for that work, which were in the thousands of dollars for each plat map, were not reasonable. He used a green highlighter to show the changed conditions on the final plat maps. These changes revealed, apparently, that very little work had been done and certainly not enough work to justify the large fees in the engineer's final invoice.

As I studied the maps that night trying to figure out what I was going to do with this testimony, I noticed that one of the maps had significantly more changes than the expert had told the jury about. The closer I looked the more changes I saw. They were substantial. The other plat map had a few additional changes though not nearly as many.

In cross-examination, after establishing that the engineer was careful and interested only in being scrupulously honest in his presentation to the jury, I drew his attention to the preliminary and final maps for the first short plat. As we identified each of the changes the developer's expert had neglected to acknowledge in his direct testimony, I asked him to highlight them with the green highlighter. It had the desired effect. When we finished with that one, the map was covered in green. Apparently, he had not been scrupulously honest in his testimony.

Then I asked, "Would it surprise you to learn this other final plat map also has changes you forgot to tell us about?"

Feeling pretty sheepish and embarrassed at this point, the witness said, "No, it would not surprise me." I left it at that. The jury could imagine what they wanted.

The jury liked my engineer client more than they liked the developer and they awarded all the fees we claimed. The court entered a judgment with attorney fees, but the developer succeeded in avoiding any payment. One reason to settle cases is that it can be much easier to get a judgment than to collect on one.

☽ ☽ ☽

I skirted close to the line once before in an injury case. The plaintiff was a hot head who said he injured his back due to my client's negligence. He had seen many doctors and therapists, and visited several clinics and hospitals, and nobody could figure out what was the problem. When I got up to cross-examine him at trial, I started by asking,

"Sir, is it a fact that you have been to see almost every single doctor and hospital in a three county area?"

Quick to anger, and with a red face, he bellowed back at me, "That is a god-damned lie!"

The jury hated his guts after that. They should have, but he was technically correct.

A lawyer is ethically bound to have a good faith basis for asking a question in trial or a deposition. It was not literally true that he had seen every single doctor and hospital in a three county area, but the list of doctors, hospitals, specialists and clinics he had visited was long and my slight exaggeration as to "almost every doctor" was close enough to true to be a fair question.

Chapter 9

The Shocking Head

Charles Gilbo would not come home for two or three days at a time. When he did come home, with bloodshot eyes and clothes that looked like he had been sleeping under a bridge, he usually did not know where he had been. That and more is how his wife told the story.

Our law firm's client manager said Allstate had a case coming up for trial and they wanted us to take the case over from the in house counsel's office. I liked these last minute trial adventures and volunteered and told him, "I'll try the case." As the Chinese proverb goes, be careful what you wish for.

This happened before. One morning about 10 am the firm's asbestos client manager called me and said, "Mike, do you want to try a case today?"

I said, "Sure, what do you have?"

"Two cases are set to start at 11 this morning. I'll tell you about them on the way to the court house and you can have your pick."

On the way down to court, he told me in one case plaintiff was living with asbestosis. We had a good doctor's report on our side and there was a statute of limitations defense. The other case was for wrongful death caused by mesothelioma and there wasn't much of a defense. I picked the asbestosis case. As my luck would have it, his case settled after the jury was seated.

My case went all the way to a verdict for plaintiff for $1.8 million. Among other challenges, our trial judge refused to instruct the jury on the statute of limitations defense.

He said, "Mr. Bond, your defense is that plaintiff does not have asbestosis. If he doesn't have asbestosis, then how can the statute of limitations have run?"

Then he ordered us to proceed with final argument after 4:30 when the court reporters, all of whom are county employees, all went home and he refused to give us time to bring in a private reporter for argument. Plaintiff's attorney, as might be expected in that circumstance with no court reporter there to take down the argument, went wild with arguments inciting the jury to punish our clients.

The first time I objected to the improper argument, the judge, who was the brother of my client in my first court appearance in King County Superior Court, said, "Mr. Bond, there is no reason to object because there is nobody to object in front of." He seemed to overlook the fact that one objects *in front of the judge* so the judge can make a ruling. For those and other questionable rulings, the court of appeals reversed the judgment and remanded for a new trial.

⅄ ⅄ ⅄

The Allstate case arose from a rear end car crash on the freeway. Our client was driving a new Cadillac when the rush hour traffic in front of him stopped suddenly. Unable to brake quickly enough, he ran into Mr. Gilbo's fifteen year old Ford Ranger pickup. My driver hit the truck hard enough to cause the Cadillac's airbag to inflate, burning my client's arms in the process. Mr. Gilbo told the investigating state trooper he bumped his head in the accident, and an ambulance transported him to the hospital. In the hospital emergency room, the doctors

147

could find no evidence of a head injury and they discharged him to go home.

He lawyered up and sued the Cadillac driver alleging damages for a closed head injury. These are tough cases because usually there is not much objective evidence to go on. The symptoms vary widely. In Mr. Gilbo's case he described spacey moments, memory loss, occasional headaches and an inability to concentrate, all of which were consistent with his wandering off for days at a time.

Allstate's in-house lawyer sent Mr. Gilbo out for an independent medical examination, known as an IME, with Dr. Cheryl Hays, and a psychological evaluation. Both examinations came back reporting no injury occurred in the accident. The defense lawyer took Mr. Gilbo's deposition but they did nothing else to work the case up for trial. Mr. Gilbo treated with a naturopathic doctor and he was making a huge earnings loss claim, but no discovery was conducted from the doctor, the employer or any of the dozen lay witnesses who were identified in the witness disclosure.

I reviewed the file with the reports, met with our client and figured, no problem, I know my way around the court house and it ought to be just as easy as those bail hearings at El Toro Marine Base my first summer of law school.

A few days after we got the case file, Mr. Gilbo's attorney filed a motion for partial summary judgment. In this motion, he argued that there was no dispute over the liability. My guy ran into the rear of Mr. Gilbo's truck on the freeway. The law says the following driver has the duty to keep a safe distance from the vehicle in front, and the State Patrol cited my guy for following too closely. Although the citation is not admissible to prove negligence, that didn't stop Mr. Gilbo's lawyer from putting it before the judge. My client said he thought he saw a raccoon run out onto the road and that is why traffic suddenly stopped. But he didn't say anything like that at the accident scene and the judge ruled my client was negligent. The only issue for trial is what damages, if any, were caused in the accident.

During trial, plaintiff's wife and a surprise witness caused some fireworks.

Mrs. Gilbo testified that when her husband came home from what sounded to me like a bender, his head literally shocked her.

She testified, "I didn't know where he had been and he couldn't recall when I asked him. He was confused. When I put my hands on his head to try to give him a massage, an electric shock hit me and almost knocked me down."

That was about the most ridiculous thing I had ever heard come from a witness on the stand. It was so silly I figured the jury must think these people are nuts. Ordinarily you don't want to ask the witness to simply repeat what they said in direct examination. Louis Nizer did it once in the Triangle Shirt Waist fire case and he succeeded in showing the jury that the witness's testimony was contrived. I decided to give it a go with Mrs. Gilbo.

On cross examination I asked, "Mrs. Gilbo would you tell the jury again about that electric shock thing?" She repeated the story.

I asked, "Was this a shock like you might get from static electricity on a dry day?"

"No, this was a shock like I put my finger in a light socket."

"Did your husband act like he was in any pain or if he felt the shock, too?"

"No."

"Where do you think the electricity came from?"

"I have no idea; I just know this never happened before he was in the accident on the freeway."

I was similarly shocked when the jury rendered its verdict.

ᴧ ᴧ ᴧ

Mr. Gilbo's attorney called the naturopathic physician who treated Gilbo for his closed head injury. Over my objection that he wasn't there and had no basis on which to say anything about it, the witness was allowed to testify that the Emergency Room doctors were so busy they failed to see the head injury.

I called our IME doctor, Dr. Hays, and the psychologist to testify. We went through Dr. Hays' qualifications, and the medical records she reviewed, and she described her examination of Mr. Gilbo in detail. All these things formed the basis of her opinion that plaintiff was not seriously injured in the accident, he suffered no injury to his head, and what injuries he had were fully resolved within six months of the accident.

Mr. Gilbo's attorney asked very specific and precise questions about things she did and said and the things Gilbo did and said in the examination. Gilbo's attorney sent a nurse to the IME and she was present throughout the examination.

After the defense rested, Mr. Gilbo's attorney called a rebuttal witness: the nurse who attended the IME. The witness was not on their witness list and they gave no information about what she might say in the interrogatories that Allstate's in house counsel had sent them. When I objected to calling this undisclosed witness, the trial judge, Bruce Hilyer, said, "Mr. Bond, your client did so little discovery, I really don't think it would have made any difference whether they disclosed her or not." He allowed the witness to testify.

Gilbo's attorney began to elicit very precise responses about the things Dr. Hays did and said and the things Gilbo did and said during the examination. For example, Dr. Hays said Gilbo could walk across the room without any change in his gait. The witness said, "That is not correct, he had a noticeable limp in his gait." After a few of these precise disputes, I objected again.

"Your honor, may we have a hearing out of the presence of the jury?"

The judge granted my request and asked the jury to return to the jury room.

I said, "These questions are in direct response to various questions that he asked of my witness and I think Mr. Gilbo's attorney must have a report from the witness."

Judge Hilyer asked the attorney, "Do you have a report?"

He said, "Yes, your honor."

I complained, "My client did serve interrogatories that asked for reports of experts and the report of this expert was not disclosed. I request the court to order production of the report to me right now, and I would like to be given a few minutes to review it before any more questions were asked of this witness." I was getting pretty worked up at this point. The judge granted my request.

When I saw the report, which was a 20 page single spaced summary of the examination, I was livid with anger. It completely disputed everything Dr. Hays said in her testimony.

When Judge Hilyer came back on the bench, I handed the report up to him. I pointed out the precise questions that were asked of Dr. Hays and I said, "Mr. Gilbo's attorney obviously used this expert report in cross examining Dr. Hays. It is grossly unfair to hide this in discovery and then use it against me later."

Judge Hilyer looked it over closely and I could sense his growing displeasure at what had transpired. Clearly the report should have been produced in discovery and it was just as clear that Mr. Gilbo's attorney concealed it only to spring it on me at trial. Then the judge did something I have not seen before or since.

Judge Hilyer pointed at the witness like an angered Moses might have done and thundered at her, "Madam, you will leave this courtroom right this minute and you will not come back."

When the jury came back into the jury box, Judge Hilyer instructed them, "You will disregard everything that witness just said. We will hear no more from her."

The following day, the jury returned a verdict for plaintiff for $1.3 million, a truly shocking outcome.

Chapter 10

Mock Juries

A tool in use today that Louis Nizer, author of *My Life in Court*, did not use is the mock jury. Mock juries are often used in high stakes cases when an aspect of the case or its evidence is difficult to evaluate. I use my wife, Marianne, in a similar capacity. She has a good nose for bullshit, and she's bold enough to tell me when it starts flying. In large cases, however, clients want more than Marianne's sniff test. That's when I might bring in a mock jury.

For a mock jury, a consultant finds folks who will come to hear the case as if they were jurors for a small fee. The lawyers work up a summary of the best case for both sides, present the evidence in an abbreviated trial format, and then watch the jury deliberate by way of a video camera set up to record the mock trial. All of this takes place without the other side knowing what you have done. It always produces useful information.

人 人 人

A mock jury was useful in one plaintiff's case. My client was driving to work one day and stopped at a traffic light when a guy plowed into the rear of his car. The collision's impact fractured my client's neck, shattering one of his cervical vertebrae and damaging another one. It was a miracle for him that the injury did not sever his spinal cord. He was a physically fit fifty year old man and got out of the car to see what happened. Aside from a sore neck, he appeared to be uninjured. After the police officer wrote up a report, the client went to work that night driving a delivery truck for a bakery. The next day my client went to the hospital where they took an x-ray and the doctor diagnosed the fractured vertebrae.

I'd handled a defense case for this client's brother several years prior to the accident. When the recovery from the accident did not go so well, they called me to see if I was interested in taking on the case. Although I usually do defense work, I've taken on every plaintiff who came to me asking for help with a just cause. It helps when the damages are substantial, as they were in this case. Without doubt it appeared to me the damages were the result of a clear case of liability.

The vertebrae were fractured in such a way that the recommended treatment was to surgically remove the vertebrae and insert a titanium cage where the vertebrae used to be. The x-rays of his neck after the surgery showed a dramatic and visible sign of the injury with this metal cage in his neck. Unfortunately, the cage in my client's neck pinched his esophagus and trachea when he looked down. It was quite an uncomfortable thing to watch when he looked down and tried to breathe or swallow. I knew this case had large damages all over it and hoped a mock jury might tell us what issues we should plan for. We would factor the results into our settlement negotiations and trial if it came to trial.

For the mock jury presentation, I played myself, and an associate played the defense lawyer. We worked out some agreed statements of what the evidence was, and the client gave a brief live testimony. We pitched the case to one jury of twelve folks.

It seemed to me that the phrase "broken neck" described the injury in powerfully graphic terms. I used that expression – broken neck – several times in presenting the evidence and in argument to the mock jury. We watched the jury deliberations by a video feed in another room. Two things became evident early on.

First, the jury seemed to question whether the at fault driver was, in fact, at fault. Several jurors tried to find arguments to show that the fellow who completely failed to stop for the red light and crashed into the rear of my client while he was minding his own business was not at fault. It had not occurred to me that liability might be an issue in the case. I concluded that we should seek a partial summary judgment on that issue as a means of foreclosing any such arguments. In a partial summary judgment, the judge would rule as a matter of law that the following driver was at fault. At the trial of the case, the jury would not be asked to decide whether the plaintiff has proven the defendant was at fault. The only issue for them to decide is the amount of damages that were caused by the accident.

Second, the jury was nearly unanimous early in the deliberations that my client could not possibly have broken his neck in the accident because, they argued, you don't walk away from a car accident with a broken neck, and you don't go to work as a truck driver with an injury like that. Several of the jurors agreed this was just common sense. A broken neck generally results in paralysis or even death. This was an issue we would want to discuss in jury selection.

In the end they arrived at a very modest damage award, which very likely was driven down by the uncertainty about the cause of injury. That happens many times. In a tough case of liability, the jury may find for the plaintiff, but think they are doing justice by making a smaller award.

In this case, the mock jury showed me I should stop saying "he broke his neck" and use language that was entirely consistent with the medical evidence, which was that "he fractured his cervical vertebrae." With this insight, we negotiated a reasonable settlement.

⅄ ⅄ ⅄

We used a mock jury in *Albano vs. Keybank.* This suit arose from the renovation of an apartment building Keybank owned. My client was the property management firm that collected the rent and hired the renovation contractors. The renovation work was to replace all the water pipes in the aging building. In order to complete the work, they were required to open up the ceilings and walls in the hallways. The ceilings and walls contained asbestos materials, and the contractors failed to take any precautions for asbestos. After the work was completed, forty-five tenants sued, claiming exposure to asbestos had caused them injury. The plaintiffs had suffered no actual injury. The claim was for emotional distress over the fear they might get cancer later in life as a result of the exposure they had when the renovation work was under way.

The plaintiffs' experts agreed there were no existing injuries and most of the debate was about the degree of chance that anyone would ever get sick. The exposure levels were so low that the chance of injury, if any, was extremely small. Again, we hoped a mock jury would give us information about how a jury might perceive these claims of injury.

We presented the case to three juries at the same time. I made the case for the plaintiffs, and each of the defense attorneys played themselves. The juries then split up into three groups and began deliberations. We set up the study to add information and questions while they deliberated.

The most interesting result was the immediacy with which all three juries attacked the bank. They said,

"That's just like a bank, especially one headquartered out of state," one juror remarked.

"Banks always do this – take your rent money and then lowball the maintenance of the property," a second juror observed.

"This bank must have known this was going to happen, they figured nobody would catch them," opined another juror.

"We need to send the home office a message that they better not do this again," yet another juror declared.

The bank's attorney was upset with me for going after the bank so fiercely in my presentation that the jury wanted blood.

ᆺ ᆺ ᆺ

In The Indian Bones case, we also used three mock juries. In this case, the Lummi Indian tribe filed suit in federal court when my archaeologist client, whose job it was to monitor the excavation of a large hole into a known Indian burial ground at a construction site in Washington State, gathered up twenty-seven sets of skeletal remains and took them to his office in Colorado.

When the Indians discovered what happened, a great commotion ensued. At one time there were three lawsuits, simultaneous state and federal criminal investigations, and one professional association investigation underway. All of these events were accompanied by extensive newspaper and television reporting. The case followed closely on the heels of the Kennewick Man controversy, where the Northwest Tribes, professional archeologists, and the Department of Interior fought over possession of an ancient skeleton found in a bluff beside the Columbia River. Several issues concerned us.

The history of our state and its Indian tribes is freighted with conflict. We had Indian wars in the 1800's, a conflict over fishing rights that was resolved just as the fishing industry began to fail, and during the past three decades, we've seen the growing presence of Indian casinos, the earnings of which have allowed some tribes to prosper. In the early 1980's Congress adopted the Native American Graves and Repatriation Act (NAGPRA), in which all museums were required to return Indian remains and artifacts from the tribes they were taken from. Against this backdrop of the nearly genocidal treatment of the Native American, our likely Seattle jury pool would consist of very liberal-minded folks, most of whom were well aware of our state's history and ashamed about it. Or so I thought.

Each side in this case had done things that could be harmful to its position. The tribe had refused to be present for the excavations because the City would not pay them a small wage. My client could have done more to provide notice to the tribe when he began to uncover human remains. The city's representatives were on site while the remains were removed and, more or less, told the archeologist to, "hurry up!"

The soil from the large excavation was taken to a local landowner's property and spread out over five acres. He had planned to build a warehouse on it. Then they discovered the excavated material was full of human remains. This was a catastrophe. The Lummi set about to sift the dirt at this site to recover their ancestors and give them a proper reburial, and they told us it would probably take five years and cost upwards of $7 million to complete the work. We were skeptical that they were in fact sifting the dirt out at the site, and so I retained an investigator to go watch the site and take photographs of what he saw. A few weeks later he called me.

"Mike, I just received a call from the FBI Special Agent in Bellingham I thought you ought to know about," the conversation started.

"What did he say, George?"

"He said, we have noticed your van out at the Freeman property for the last couple of weeks. What are you doing?"

This site was about a half mile as the crow flies from the Cherry Point oil refinery and these events occurred about three months after the September 11 terrorist attack. It was mildly comforting to know the government was doing more than checking out elderly ladies with blue hair at the airport while watching for bad guys.

I said, "George, I told you that Praise Allah bumper sticker was going to get you in trouble someday."

The investigation did show that the Lummi were on site nearly every day sifting the earth for remains.

人 人 人

It was difficult to predict what impact each side's story would have on a jury's decision to impose liability or not, and if so, what they would award as the damages.

We videotaped two presentations, one for the plaintiff and one for the defendants. I played the role of plaintiff's attorney and pulled out all stops in condemning the gross violations of the contracts, reasonable care, and human decency. One of my partners took on the role of the defense attorney and made what arguments we had. After presenting the arguments to the juries, we watched the deliberations from another room.

The most striking aspect of the deliberations was the explicit racism that was revealed. On each of the three juries, which were randomly assembled, at least one person spoke of the Indians in derogatory terms. They said things like, "It's just like the Indians, to lie in the weeds and jump up and ambush you with the latest grievances." "When will they have enough?" "They got all the fish and now they want the land back, too."

These sentiments were countered by several jurors who spoke about the violation of law and the sordid history of the treatment of the Native Americans. These jurors wondered how the archeologist had the gall to take the bones to Colorado when he had to drive right past the Lummi Reservation on his way out of town.

The three juries arrived at very different damage awards from a very low award to one for several million dollars. What we learned from the mock juries was the case had explosive potential, and we ended up settling the claims for a very large sum.

Chapter 11

I Am Sorry

S ometimes a simple apology can be worth more than gold. In many cases, by the time two parties reach the point when a lawsuit is filed, a large amount of emotion including anger, resentment, and ill will has been felt on all sides. Good lawyers keep an eye out for the chance to reach closure with an apology.

In *Illich vs. Pope Resources* a simple apology made all the difference.

Wilma Illich and her husband, a happily retired couple who lived in Montana, were visiting their daughter in the Seattle area when they decided to play a round of golf at the resort at Port Ludlow. The golf course there is beautiful and challenging, built into a second-growth forest owned by Pope Resources, a timber company. The resort's terrain of rolling hills is covered with large trees making it difficult to see one hole from another. One hole has a periscope so golfers can see where their ball went down the fairway. An internationally acclaimed golf course designer, Robert Muir Graves, designed the golf course.

Ms. Illich, who didn't play golf, drove the cart for her husband. Unfortunately, on this day she had trouble with the cart's brake system. The golf cart had a typical brake with a little side pedal on the brake that would hold the cart still when you pressed on it hard enough and set the brake. On the front nine holes, she just could not make the brake work the way she wanted. The brake would seize up and stop the cart with a skid. To remedy that problem, she told us she decided to avoid using the brake on the back nine and, instead, let the engine slow the cart to a stop.

The tee box on the tenth hole at Port Ludlow is separated from the fairway by a deep gully. Golfers hit for the fairway across what seems like the Grand Canyon. With skill or luck or both you can clear the gully. I usually used to take a mulligan on that hole.

Wilma's husband made a clean drive well onto the fairway, and they jumped into the cart to head to the fairway for the next stroke. The cart path descends steeply into the gully. At the bottom of the gully the path makes a sharp left turn where it crosses a wooden bridge, and then it climbs another steep path to reach the fairway.

While descending the cart path, Wilma's cart began to pick up speed. Taking her foot off the gas didn't slow the cart down. As she approached the turn, she just knew she wasn't going to be able to make the corner without tipping over. She saw an escape route. Where the cart path turned left, the path appeared to run out straight and flat into the bushes. She figured she could avoid the turn and just run the cart up into the bushes and stop safely, like one of those runaway truck exits you see on the freeway. Unfortunately, the bushes concealed a fir tree about three feet in diameter and she ran the cart headfirst into the tree at high speed. Wilma was thrown forward and her waist hit the steering wheel and the force of the impact broke her back. She fell out of the cart and onto the ground, paralyzed from the waist down.

⅄ ⅄ ⅄

Right after the golf course construction was completed, the resort's liability insurance company had hired a traffic engineer to inspect the course for safety hazards. The traffic engineer's report noted that the cart path on the tenth hole descended sharply into the gully. The path was very steep, and the engineer recommended erecting a warning sign about the sharp turn at the bottom of the path. The resort manager put the report in a drawer. He moved on to another job a few weeks later and forgot all about the report. Nothing was done about the report's recommendations.

After Wilma and her husband filed suit for her injuries, the engineer's report was produced in discovery. Bill Spencer represented the resort. He told me he knew his client was doomed as soon as he saw the report, and he had no alternative other than to produce it in discovery. The report all but guaranteed the resort would pay for Wilma Illich's accident even though one might argue her contributory negligence for failing to use the cart brake was the only cause of her accident. After all, you could see the path was steep.

⋏ ⋏ ⋏

In order to prove a case against the golf course designer, plaintiff would have to show a breach of a professional duty of care, which usually requires expert testimony. Ms. Illich's attorneys hired a local golf course designer to prove up the case. Or so I thought. In preparing for the expert's deposition, I could find no information about him, other than some very limited information that was shown on his website.

I took his deposition. After exploring his background, what information he had reviewed, and what might be the basis for any opinion he was going to offer against my client, I asked,

"Do you have any opinion as to whether the design of the golf course met or fell below the standard of care expected of a reasonably careful golf course designer?"

He said, "Well, I think this course was beautifully designed."

I said, "I am sure Mr. Graves will be happy to hear that, and I'll pass it on, but what about the standard of care of golf course designers? Do have any opinions about that?"

He said, "Yes, I think the design showed careful attention to every standard of care."

Somewhat flabbergasted, but thankful nonetheless for that testimony, I asked, "Well, sir, then why are we here? Why did you take this case as an expert witness?"

He said, "I just wanted the chance to meet Mr. Graves. I have his book and have admired his work for many years." I looked at Ms. Illich's lawyer and wondered why he let it get this far.

We filed a motion for summary judgment, but the federal judge assigned to the case denied the motion. He thought the traffic engineer's report created an issue of fact about whether the golf course design complied with all relevant standards.

⅄ ⅄ ⅄

We set up a mediation to try to settle the case. The resort would no doubt have to pay its insurance policy limits, even though Wilma's contributory negligence in failing to use the brakes could result in no jury award if the case were tried. But obviously paralysis was a serious injury, and a jury would be likely to sympathize with her plight. It can be very dangerous to roll the dice in a case like this. In preparing for the mediation, Mr. Graves asked me if he could speak to the plaintiff. He said he felt badly that she had been hurt on one of his golf courses.

Lots of injuries happen on golf courses. Usually, players or guests are injured by flying golf balls, or a golfer gets whacked by standing too close to his playing partner, but this was different.

It occurred to me that a simple apology would help both of them to get beyond what happened. Wilma knew she had blown it and would live with the result of her poor judgment for the rest of her life. While there was no defect in the golf course design, Mr. Graves thought he should say something to her to help her if he could.

I asked Wilma's lawyer ahead of time if it would be acceptable if Mr. Graves spoke to his client and he agreed to let him speak with her. At the beginning of the mediation, I gave Mr. Graves a signal, and he walked over to where she had parked her wheelchair. He took her hand and leaned in so close I couldn't hear what he said, but I am sure it was something like, "Mrs. Illich, I am very sorry you were hurt on one of my golf courses." She thanked him and looked up at me with tears in her eyes.

Later in the day, the case settled. The resort agreed to pay its insurance policy limits, and my client's insurer agreed to pay a sum that was less than half of what it would have cost to try the case.

When we parted ways for the last time, Mr. Graves thanked me for letting him speak to Wilma Illich; it gave him closure. The trial lawyer should always look for ways to reduce the impact of bad breaks on our clients, and sometimes all it may take is a chance to say I am sorry.

Chapter 12

In Defense of Dithering Nincompoops[1]

On more than one occasion in my sixty-two years of being a guy with opinions, I am sure that somebody has thought of me as a nincompoop, other than my wife and children, of course. Indeed, far less charitable labels were cast my way in 2008 when I got it in my head that I should run for election as a Justice on our State Supreme Court. But a recent decision of our Court shows that nincompoops are in sorry need of an advocate. Volunteering once again, I am ready to serve.

Nincompoops – "dithering" nincompoops to be specific – made an appearance in *State vs. Jaime*, which the Washington Supreme Court decided on May 27, 2010. The issue in the case was whether the trial of a man accused of murder should have been conducted in the jailhouse, which was across the street from the Yakima County Courthouse. I know from several appearances in the Yakima County Courthouse that while the building is not an architectural beauty, it is a serviceable and dignified place in which justice is administered. But in Mr. Jaime's case, the prosecution thought the defendant was such a dangerous man and the risk of escape or violence or other untoward event sufficiently great that it would be better if the trial was conducted in the jailhouse across the street from the courthouse. The trial judge agreed with the prosecution, over the vigorous objection of Mr. Jaime's lawyers.

Mr. Jaime's lawyers argued that conducting the trial in the jailhouse would have a negative impact on the presumption of

---

[1] A prior version of this story appeared in the Washington State Bar Journal in September, 2010.

innocence which is, of course, said to be a bedrock foundation of our democracy. I am setting aside for the purposes of my point here that one might query whether the presumption of innocence is more fiction than fact, in view of the way some minorities and all air travelers are treated. As might have been anticipated, Mr. Jaime was convicted of murder. The Supreme Court reversed his conviction, holding that conducting a trial in the jailhouse would be expected to have an impact on the presumption of innocence and was, therefore, a denial of due process.

Three justices dissented, including the one I ran against in 2008, and Justice Jim Johnson's dissenting opinion introduced us to dithering nincompoops. Justice Johnson's argument was that jurors are smart enough to know that the presumption of innocence is not, should not, and will not be affected by the location of the trial, and he rallied behind the well-known intelligence and wisdom of the ordinary juror. He said, "Our system of laws depends upon the assumption that jurors are intelligent," and he quoted the opinion of a California Court of Appeals, which said: "A juror is not some kind of dithering nincompoop, brought in from never-never land and exposed to the harsh realities of life for the first time in the jury box," citing *People vs. Barnum*, 104 Cal. Rptr. 2d 19, 24 (Cal. Ct. App. 2001).

Now, I'm one of the biggest advocates of the common sense of the common man and woman, but I also know from many jury trials in thirty-plus years of trial practice that jurors *can* be dithering nincompoops who reside in never-never land and are exposed to the harsh realities of life for the first time in the jury box. Some jurors are very intelligent and well-educated, but others can barely read and quite possibly have not been taught to think for themselves. Some jurors follow all current events, but others know nothing or next to nothing about life. Some jurors are aware of what goes on in their communities and others seem to live in a never-never land.

In fact, during my ill-fated judicial campaign I encountered several folks from never-never land in the 36th Legislative District, and there was this one fellow from Eastern Washington.

I used my cell phone as the campaign headquarters telephone. It was useful because the voters were pleasantly surprised to speak to the candidate whenever they wanted to talk. And usually I was not reluctant to tell them what I thought. On the day of the election I received a call from Chewelah, which is in Northeast Washington; many folks out there live off the grid and some may still be fighting the Indians. He said, "I'm in the polling place and I'm trying to decide who to vote for."

I said, "That's great, thanks for your call, sir, what can I do for you?"

He asked, "What do you think about the Second Amendment?" Many voters asked me this question. My opponent, the incumbent, was decidedly opposed to firearms.

I replied, "I am a gun owner and I like the Second Amendment."

He quickly said, "That's good enough for me," and he hung up. In thinking about it, I am no longer sure if he voted for me or not.

So I say, let's not pretend the dithering nincompoops are not out there. As the wise philosopher, Pogo, once said, "I have met the enemy and he is us."

Chapter 13

Burden on My Shoulders

One aspect of the trial lawyer's practice that I learned about early on repeated itself throughout my career. It happened again while having lunch with a friend who has a large pile of problems and is trying to hang on to his business. Some of his troubles are self-inflicted, no doubt. Some resulted from the flagging economy, some by employees who were less careful than they should have been, and some were just bad luck. Several years ago he and his wife adopted two children, and then his wife died unexpectedly shortly afterwards. He's been a single dad ever since. Then a couple of months ago his fourteen-year-old daughter informed him she wants to be a boy, with hormone treatment and surgery – the whole nine yards. He does not know what to do, if anything. Good grief, neither do I.

Friends come to me often asking me to represent them in a legal dispute. As a general rule I decline to represent my friends; there are too many opportunities to lose objectivity, and when you cannot tell the friend what they want to hear, you can lose that friend. I found it is better to refer your friends to a good lawyer.

Lawyers are like doctors because sometimes it seems like all we see are sick people. After handling construction cases for thirty years, I am amazed that any building gets built without a catastrophe of some kind. After a career dealing with the claims of widows, widowers, victims of horrible disfiguring injuries, burns, quadriplegic injury, and all sorts of cancers, it's a miracle I don't suffer from post-traumatic stress disorder. Maybe I do.

If so, that is only because I care about people. You shouldn't do this work if you don't care about people.

In the privacy of our offices, the clients share their innermost problems and fears. What we can do is listen. Sometimes that's all we can do. Sometimes we can do more.

One time in the Marines, the client and his wife came to tell me they were childless. They were going through the interview process necessary to adopt a child. They were concerned about the pending court martial – on charges so ridiculous it is unbelievable – and they were profoundly worried about what might happen to their plans for adoption if the husband had a federal court criminal conviction on his record. They wanted children and adoption was the only way that was going to happen. I immediately went over to see the convening authority. He said I was on a "mission of mercy," and before I left his office he called the First Sergeant and told him to withdraw the charges. That dilemma was resolved.

Once an officer told me that his first job in Vietnam was to go through a battlefield and kill the wounded enemy. I sat there wondering why he was telling me this because it sounded like a war crime to me. I concluded that he needed to tell someone and I was his chosen audience. Once chosen there is no escape. The stories kept coming.

Grown men and women cry. One afternoon during my judicial campaign I was walking back to my office after a great radio show interview. The sun was shining and everything was going my way when my cell phone rang. An older woman had called.

She started out by asking me, "Do you favor capital punishment?" Although usually I was not bashful about stating my views, I tried to duck and dodge that question because I oppose capital punishment, and it is very popular in our state. At least it was then.

I replied, "Well ma'am it is the law of this state."

She said, "But you haven't answered my question." She was right, of course. So I said, "My job as a judge would be to apply the law even if I don't like it."

She changed the question, "Well why are there so many men on death row who haven't been executed, yet?"

Seeing an escape door, I hurried toward it and said, "You can blame the federal judges for that."

Then she changed the question again by asking me about myself. I told her, "I have two children and I was a Marine officer in my former life." The military service always played well with the more conservative voters.

She said, "I had six children and my youngest was a Marine."

Missing the past tense in that statement, I said, "That is terrific, what does he do now."

Then she said, "He was 19 when he was killed in Vietnam." And then she began to cry. She still carried with her until that moment all the grief that she had felt 50 years ago when her son died. Losing a child is said to be one of worst possible life experiences, and hearing her grief come through my cell phone took all the sunshine out of my day.

I tell all new clients to be aware of the stress associated with being in a lawsuit, especially one in which your client's negligence is said to have ruined a business, resulted in a death, or left someone confined to a wheelchair for the rest of their lives. I've seen the stress of litigation destroy colleagues' marriages, partnerships and long-standing friendships.

That's the way it is in this job. New lawyers should steel themselves for what will come: sad stories, shame, embarrassment, anger, and skeletons stashed so deep in the closet they would never see the light of day if that man or woman had not come into your office one day asking for help. My advice to you is learn to listen, and try not to judge.

λ λ λ

If you keep the following suggestions in mind, the trial lawyer's life will be less complicated.

1. Pat Cook taught me there is no such thing as a small case; to every client, being sued for small damages is as important as the big ones, especially for those who haven't been down the road before.

2. The client may not tell you the truth and this happens for many reasons. They may not know the truth, they may think they have to keep it a secret, they may be an inveterate liar, and they may think they know the truth and in fact do not. Those are usually the most difficult persons to deal with.

3. The client may confess to a civil crime they did not commit; this may happen because they feel bad someone got hurt and take responsibility for it when legally they are not at fault; they may apply the terminology of duty and breach in inaccurate ways; they may not have all the information that they would need in order to judge themselves more accurately; they may judge themselves by a standard of perfection that the law does not require.

4. The client often thinks that the lawyer is out to make a pile of money and really doesn't care about the client's welfare. Maybe some do, but all the good lawyers I know care about the client's predicament.

5. The client will only recall and sometimes only hear the things he or she wants to hear, and this is why it is important to communicate all important matters in writing.

6. The largest error the lawyer can make is to exhibit arrogance; lawyers are not the smartest, cleverest, or wisest humans on earth and those who act like it do their clients and themselves a disservice.

7. It is the client's lawsuit and not the lawyer's; so do what the client wants, and if the client refuses to follow your advice and you can't deal with it, then withdraw.

8. If you are retained by an insurer, remember that the person you are defending is the client, not the insurance company, and your duty is to the client and not the insurer; I always explain that to new clients. Obtain written consent to represent the client.

9. Give the client your independent best judgment and let the chips fall where they may. Not every case is a winner. Those are the cases where it is best to ask for a large advance on the fees; it can be very difficult to collect a large fee from a client who lost badly at trial.

10. Except in very rare instances, the only thing at stake is money and money isn't going to make it (whatever happened) go away. So try not to get on your high horse about the injustice of it all or exacting revenge or making the ones who did it change their ways.

11. By the time a coverage issue comes to the defense lawyer, the issues and facts usually are well known to the insurer. I prefer to know what the issues are as a means of better understanding if my client is telling me a whopper or is about to do something that will make his situation even more precarious.

12. Inform the client that the process takes a long time to reach conclusion and they should find a way to set the matter aside and not worry about it. I've seen suits ruin marriages and partnerships because the principals did not know how to "leave it at the office."

13. Avoid at all costs surprising the client at the last minute with bad news. Personally deliver bad news, don't ask the secretary or paralegal or associate to do it for you. Whatever happens, make sure the client doesn't learn about it first in the newspaper.

⋏ ⋏ ⋏

I learned about a valuable tool for dealing with these heavy responsibilities from Murray Kleist, who was one of the stalwarts of the plaintiff's trial bar. It was his unlucky break to try the *Chaussee vs. Maryland Casualty* case I wrote about in Chapter Three: A Case of Bad Faith. Judge McCutcheon was giving Murray no breaks at all during the trial, over-ruling most of his objections and granting most of ours. When he launched into an argument with the judge, Murray would flap his arms up and down. We had a wager about how long it would be before he actually levitated off the ground. In Murray's summation to the jury, after finishing the analysis of the evidence, the facts and the law, all of which showed the plaintiff should prevail, he said,

"You may have noticed during this trial that I care about these people. Representing them is a great burden on my shoulders. They come to me asking for my help, and I do everything in my power to help them. I take my responsibility to these folks very seriously. It weighs heavily on my shoulders. But this is the part of the trial that enables me to keep doing this work."

And then he touched his shoulders as if lifting something heavy, and he moved his hands toward the jury, saying, "Because now it is my pleasure to hand this burden over to you. Be careful with it. Thank you."

I have used this closing remark many times since then. It reminds the jury of the importance of their task, and it helps me deal with the burden on my shoulders.

Thank you, Murray.

Epilogue

In hindsight, it could be that I entered the practice of law in something of a golden age. In the mid 1970's law schools were anxious to admit new students, tuition was relatively inexpensive, and in 1982 when I was getting out of the Marines there were plenty of firms, companies and institutions hiring freshly minted lawyers. When I applied for my first position after the Marines, I printed up 50 resumes. When we arrived in Seattle, I interviewed on a Thursday, was offered a job on Friday, and started working at the firm the following Monday. I had 49 resumes left when I landed an associate's position. When I graduated from Gonzaga, my student debt was $7,500, and all my classmates found work practicing law if they wanted. Today many men and women graduate from law school with six figure debts and rewarding employment is much more difficult to come by. While I've been very lucky in many ways, I firmly believe you make your luck happen.

人 人 人

I hope you found these stories to be interesting and useful. It took me over 30 years to learn these things. Some of these ideas were not my own, but I learned by watching others try cases or reading the stories of great lawyers who tried cases. And I was never afraid to be creative and try something new.

I used to say I liked to lead with my chin, but that's a silly and inaccurate thing to say. I lead with my left, give the knockout punch with my right, and when the other guy is bigger and stronger I try to remember to duck.

Printed in Great Britain
by Amazon.co.uk, Ltd.,
Marston Gate.